D0873227

ABORTION
& the Early Church

*Christian, Jewish & Pagan Attitudes
in the Greco-Roman World*

Michael J. Gorman

Paulist
Press

Published by Paulist Press; Editorial Office: 1865 Broadway, New York, NY 10023; Business Office: 545 Island Road, Ramsey, NJ 97446.

All Bible quotations, unless otherwise indicated, are from the Revised Standard Version of the Bible, copyrighted 1946, 1952, © 1971 and 1973 by the Division of Christian Education of the National Council of the Churches of Christ in the USA, and are used by permission.

ISBN 0-8091-2511-0

Printed in the United States of America

Library of Congress Cataloging in Publication Data

Gorman, Michael J., 1955-
    Abortion & the early church.

    Bibliography: p.
    Includes index.
    1. Abortion–Religious aspects–Christianity–
History.   2.   Civilization, Greco-Roman.   3.   Civilization,
Pagan.   4.   Abortion–Religious aspects–Judaism–
History.   I.   Title.   II.   Title: Abortion and the early
church.
HQ767.G62   1982b   363.4'6   82-18842
ISBN 0-8091-2511-0

| 18 | 17 | 16 | 15 | 14 | 13 | 12 | 11 | 10 | 9 | 8 | 7 | 6 | 5 | 4 | 3 | 2 | 1 |
| 96 | 95 | 94 | 93 | 92 | 91 | 90 | 89 | 88 | 87 | 86 | 85 | 84 | 83 | 82 | | | |

To Nancy and Mark

FOREWORD

The study of the thinking and practice of the early church, though often neglected by modern Protestants, frequently provides the Christian today with valuable insights and information. For one thing, such study deepens one's appreciation of the strength of religious convictions that enabled believers of that age to stand firmly against conforming to the ethics and mores of the surrounding culture. Especially noteworthy in this respect was the opposition of the early church to contemporary practices of abortion. It is really remarkable how uniform and how pronounced was the early Christian opposition to abortion.

The nucleus of the present book (chapters one, two, four and five) was written as a research paper for a course on the Life and Letters of the Early Church. At my suggestion Mr. Gorman revised and enlarged his paper into the present form for publication. He has had an eye upon two kinds of readers. On the one hand, for those readers who might otherwise be mystified at the mention of the Septuagint, the Mishnah, and other such terms, he has incorporated brief descriptive explanations, as well as the dates of ancient authors. On the other hand, for those who may wish to find more specialized information by consulting the original sources, specific documentation is provided throughout in the notes. Both types of readers will, I am confident, be grateful to Mr. Gorman for having written a comprehensive, yet concise, treatment of the question of abortion and the early church.

Bruce M. Metzger
Professor of New Testament Language and Literature
Princeton Theological Seminary
Princeton, New Jersey

ACKNOWLEDGMENTS

This book could not have been completed without the assistance and support of many people. I wish to extend my gratitude especially to Professor Bruce Metzger, who first aroused my interest in the subject, encouraged me along the way and provided many helpful comments as he read the manuscript at several stages. He was also kind enough to write the foreword during a very busy time of the year. I wish to thank Professor Kathleen McVey for her insightful comments without which the book would be much poorer. My friend Heidi Stobbart kindly donated her time and talent to assist in some of the translation. Many other friends and my parents have encouraged me during trying times, and I thank them. Finally, I am deeply grateful to my wife, Nancy, for her encouragement, understanding and assistance in researching, typing and editing the book, and to our son, Mark, who was very patient with a busy daddy.

Ascension Day
1982

1
ABORTION IN THE ANCIENT WORLD

EVER SINCE THE 1973 SUPREME COURT decision that made abortion legal in all fifty states, the Christian church has been debating the issue. Is abortion ever acceptable? If so, under what circumstances? Who should make the final decision? Is abortion a sectarian issue, one where freedom of conscience should be preserved? Or is it an issue for which all of society is responsible?

Twentieth-century Christians are divided. Those who most vocally attach the name *Christian* to their position call themselves *pro-life*, but many influential Christian groups are just as ardently *pro-choice*. It is confusing to the layperson when experts disagree; what is especially troubling in this case is that the experts cannot hear each other's arguments.

Each side's apparent insensitivity to the other is not necessarily due to ignorance or ill will. Two factors seem to be at work.

First, the two sides emphasize different values: life and freedom. In any abortion decision, the values may clash. Each side seems to believe that its chosen value has priority over that of the other side. Second, neither side has been especially consistent in applying its chosen value to other areas of ethical concern. This inconsistency fuels the rhetorical fires of the opposing side, and the argument goes on.

One potential source of aid is almost never consulted. Abortion seems so obviously a twentieth-century problem that examining historical documents would appear to be a waste of time. Modern Christians may study Old Testament warfare or early Christian pacifism or the medieval just war theory to inform their discussion of nuclear war, but it is obvious that ancient Greeks and Romans did not have vacuum extractors or morning-after pills. What could the early church possibly have had to say about abortion?

Surprisingly, abortion was not at all uncommon two thousand years ago. Early Christians were forced to develop both an appropriate attitude to their culture's practice and a standard for life within the Christian community. Their statements on abortion will not, of course, provide automatic answers for all of today's ethical questions, yet no study of abortion can be complete without reference to the legacy of Christian thought that the church has preserved.

It is impossible to understand Christian attitudes and practices without first investigating abortion in its Greco-Roman context.

Motives for Abortion

From the earliest days of ancient Greece and Rome to the time of Augustine, abortion was practiced frequently by pagans and occasionally by Jews and Christians. It seems to have been more common among the wealthy than among the poor: Juvenal wrote of how seldom a "gilded bed" contained a pregnant woman because abortion was so readily available to the rich.[1] But the poor aborted too, as did married and unmarried, chaste and prostitute. Other people besides pregnant women were involved in abortion. A husband or lover might force a woman to abort. Certain doctors performed nontherapeutic as well as therapeutic abortions. Amateur and paid abortionists and dealers in abortifacient drugs were available.[2]

Motives for obtaining an abortion were no less varied in antiquity than they are today. By far the most frequent reason was to conceal illicit sexual activity. Rich women did not want to share their wealth with lower-class children fathered illegitimately.[3] Another reason was to preserve "sex appeal," for many women, especially the rich, did not enjoy the effects of pregnancy on their figures, preferring not to "get big and trouble the womb with bouncing babes."[4] As Chrysostom said of prostitutes, they had "a view of drawing more money by being agreeable and an object of longing to [their] lovers."[5] Both Plato and Aristotle recommended family limitation by abortion (if necessary), and the declines in population of the Roman Empire at the time of Augustus and again after Hadrian were probably due in part to such action by both rich and poor.[6] The wealthy did not want to share their estates with many offspring,[7] while the poor felt unable to support large families. Justinian's *Digest* mentions a woman who aborted after a divorce in order not to have a child by the man she then hated.[8] Abortion was also a corrective to the many inefficient means of contraception.[9] Finally, abortions for therapeutic reasons were performed.[10]

Methods of Abortion
Women who wanted abortions, for whatever reason, had a great variety of means available to them. Most of the techniques can be classified as either chemical or mechanical.

Chemical or medicinal abortifacients of various compositions were common.[11] Most common of all, according to the gynecologist Soranos of Ephesus, were pessaries, or substances introduced directly into the womb via the birth canal. Some of these destroyed the fetus, whereas others caused its expulsion from the womb.[12] The physician Galen wrote that certain drugs could "destroy the embryo or rupture certain of its membranes" and lead to an abortion, perhaps alone or else by using additional chemical or physical means.[13]

Besides using pessaries, women took oral drugs, or "poisons" as they were frequently labeled. Medical experts of the Roman Empire, like Soranos and Dioscorides, wrote of various plant potions used as abortifacients. For example, mixtures of wine with various combinations of wallflower seed, myrtle, myrhh, white pepper or cabbage blossoms were believed to be effective in the early stages of pregnancy.[14] Celsus named "four grams of ammoniac salt," "four grams of Cretan dittany in water" and "hedge mustard in tepid wine . . . on an empty stomach" as aids to expulsion of a dead fetus or to childbirth.[15] These or similar compounds were certainly used also for later abortions. Also in the first century A.D. the learned Pliny listed certain potions which supposedly caused abortions, but his ideas must be examined closely; he also knew of abortifacient odors (such as the dragon plant or the smell of lamps being put out) and fumes ("from an ass's house") and items which caused abortion merely on sight (certain plants, animals and parts of reproductive systems).[16] Since some of what this knowledgeable author said is pure myth, he shows that abortion with drugs was not a perfected science or skill. In fact, some supposed contraceptives were probably actually abortifacients (and vice versa), and some supposed abortifacients were undoubtedly useless.[17] Nevertheless, it was the genius of one first-century B.C. poet, Eubius, to put prescriptions for abortive potions into verse. No more useful than some potions were the charms sold by magicians and the predictions made by astrologers about good and bad days for procuring an abortion.[18]

Mechanical abortion techniques were often used instead of or as supplements to drugs. The crudest method, used most often by (probably desperate) women themselves, was to bind

the body tightly around the womb or to strike it so as to expel
the fetus.[19] Another method required the use of abortive instruments. Two of these instruments were described by Tertullian.
The first was a "copper needle or spike" such as those possessed
by Hippocrates, Asclepiades, Erasistratus, Herophilus and
Soranos. The second tool, more sophisticated but very dangerous, required a delicate surgical operation:

Among surgeons' tools there is a certain instrument, which
is formed with a nicely-adjusted flexible frame for opening the
uterus first of all, and keeping it open; it is further furnished
with an annular blade [*anulocultro*], by means of which the
limbs within the womb are dissected with anxious but un-
faltering care; its last appendage being a blunted or covered
hook, wherewith the entire *foetus* is extracted by a violent
delivery.[20]

This surgical method of abortion is undoubtedly similar to the
method of removing a dead fetus in the third trimester described
by Celsus in *De medicina:*

An operation must be done, which may be counted among
the most difficult; for it requires both extreme caution and
neatness, and entails very great risk.... The surgeon...
should first insert the index finger of his greased hand, and
keep it there until the mouth is opened again, and then he
should insert a second finger, and the other fingers on the like
opportunity, until the whole hand can be put in.... But when
the hand has reached the dead foetus its position is immediately felt.... If the head is nearest, a hook must be inserted
which is completely smooth, with a short point, and this it is
right to fix into an eye or ear or the mouth, even at times into
the forehead, then this is pulled upon and extracts the foetus.
... Now the right hand should pull the hook whilst the left
is inserted within and pulls the foetus, and at the same time
guides it.... But if the foetus is lying crosswise and cannot be
turned straight, the hook is to be inserted into an armpit and
traction slowly made; during this the neck is usually bent

back, and the head turned backwards to the rest of the foetus. The remedy then is to cut through the neck, in order that the two parts may be extracted separately. This is done with a hook which resembles the one mentioned above, but has all its inner edge sharp. Then we must proceed to extract the head first, then the rest, for if the larger portion be extracted first, the head slips back into the cavity of the womb, and cannot be extracted without the greatest risk. . . . There are also other difficulties, which make it necessary to cut up and extract a foetus which does not come out whole.[21]

The danger of these methods certainly contributed to the sensitivity of many writers to the practice of abortion. Nevertheless, a woman who wanted or was forced to abort had several options to choose from, and the medical technology of her day would be able, according to Pliny, to provide an abortion from the tenth day after conception into the seventh month of pregnancy, though abortions in that month were nearly always fatal to the mother.[22]

If abortion two thousand years ago was more dangerous for the woman than it is in today's well-equipped clinics, it was nevertheless readily available and widely practiced at the time the Christian church was born. As might be expected, church leaders had something to say about it. But before turning to their observations, we will look at the attitude toward abortion held by their non-Christian contemporaries.

2
THE PAGAN
WORLD

ABORTION MAY NOT HAVE BEEN EASY or safe for a woman in ancient times, but it was nevertheless widely practiced. Before looking at writings from the Christian era, we will examine their legal and philosophical background as found in ancient Greek and Roman documents.

Ancient Greece
Abortion was a subject of Greek legal, medical, philosophical and religious concern. Only a few of these writings remain, however, and some opinions are preserved only in the works of later authors; a precise understanding of Greek opinion and practice is consequently quite difficult.

Evidence concerning ancient Greek legal practice and opinion is unfortunately sparse. Only one source explicitly mentions antiabortion legislation in classical Greece, and scholars disagree about its reliability. According to this text, incorrectly ascribed to the second-century A.D. Roman physician Galen, both Lycurgus (the legendary ninth-century B.C. Spartan lawgiver) and Solon (the sixth-century B.C. Athenian lawgiver) prohibited abortion.[1] If the pseudo-Galen text is not based on firsthand knowledge of ancient law codes, it may nevertheless reflect later codes based on ancient statutes.[2] It is also possible that a late Stoic text refers to ancient laws.[3]

Since the exposure of newborns, however, was very common in Greece and not only went unpunished but was even expected in certain cases, it is highly unlikely that abortion of the unborn was punished.[4] If any laws against abortion did exist in classical Greece they were probably motivated out of concern for the safety of the woman or the right of the husband.

With the expansion of Greek civilization throughout the Mediterranean world, non-Greek cultures began to interact with Greek thought and life. Egyptian laws favoring the unborn child may have influenced Greek and Jewish law in Alexandria, although evidence for such influence is inconclusive.[5]

Evidence for ancient Greek medical opinion is similarly scarce. The Oath of Hippocrates (460-357 B.C.), however, included a definite promise not to perform an abortion:

> I swear by Apollo Physician, by Asclepius, by Health, by Panacea, and by all the gods and goddesses, making them my witnesses, that I will carry out, according to my ability and judgment, this oath and this indenture.... I will use treatment to help the sick according to my ability and judgment, but never with a view to injury and wrong-doing. Neither will I administer a poison to anybody when asked to do so, nor will I suggest such a course. Similarly, I will not give to a woman a pessary to cause abortion.[6]

It is unclear to modern scholars where the Oath originated, who actually composed it and, most important, who subscribed to it. The last question is significant even if the text is by Hippocrates:

the seriousness with which the Oath was written and taken has been questioned by some who find evidence that Hippocrates himself indicated means of abortion for those who wanted it.[7] Nevertheless, it is generally agreed that most Greek physicians opposed all nontherapeutic abortions.[8] An abortive pessary was seen as a poison and rejected as an attack not so much on the fetus as on the woman.

Whatever the source and integrity of the Oath, it won acceptance among Jews, Christians and Arabs; survived the Renaissance and Enlightenment with the approval of both ages; and stands as a testimony to the main, if not the only, Greek medical opinion.[9]

If medical ethics opposed abortion, social and philosophical ethics to some extent endorsed it. The "Greeks enjoy the dubious distinction of being the first [in the Ancient Near East or Western world] positively to advise and even demand abortion in certain cases."[10] In discussing the role of women in his ideal *Republic*, Plato (427-347 B.C.) commanded abortion for women who conceived after a proposed cutoff age of forty:

A woman, I said, at twenty years of age may begin to bear children to the State, and continue to bear them until forty. ... And we grant all this, accompanying the permission with strict orders to prevent any [subsequent] embryo which may come into being from seeing the light; and if any force a way to the birth, the parents must understand that the offspring of such an union can not be maintained, and arrange accordingly.[11]

Here Plato recommends both abortion and infanticide when "necessary." Although he believed that the fetus is a living being,[12] the state's ideals and needs take precedence over the life and rights of the unborn.[13]

Aristotle (384-322 B.C.) proposed a similar plan in his *Politics*. After introducing his subject (books 1-3) and discussing political realities (books 4-6), Aristotle revealed his "ideal" politics (books 7-8), "the most desirable form of life" for the individual and the state.[14] To produce the finest human material, the state must regulate marriage: marital age, number and spacing of children, physical conditions for procreation and pregnancy, and quality of children. In that context he writes:

> Let there be a law that no deformed child shall be reared; but on the ground of number of children, if the regular customs hinder any of those born being exposed, there must be a limit fixed to the procreation of offspring, and if any people have a child as a result of intercourse in contravention of these regulations, abortion must be practised on it before it has developed sensation and life; for the line between lawful and unlawful abortion will be marked by the fact of having sensation and being alive.[15]

Aristotle calls for the accepted practice of infant exposure (abandonment to death) but realizes that others will not always agree; he nevertheless demands a limit to family size. Once the limit is potentially surpassed by a new pregnancy, however, abortion becomes compulsory in his ideal society.

Though Aristotle in the *Politics* did distinguish between "lawful and unlawful" abortions based on whether or not the fetus was alive, in that work he did not provide criteria for determining this. According to another of his works, life is present in a fetus when distinct organs have been formed: forty days after conception for males, ninety days for females.[16] His distinguishing between a fetus with sensation and life and one without finds parallels in other philosophers and in the Greek Septuagint version of Exodus 21:22-23, sources which influenced some later Christian writings. Aristotle's differentiation was made fundamentally from a legal perspective, however, not from a moral perspective as later occurred among the Christians he influenced.

Why did both Plato and Aristotle support abortion? It is highly unlikely that either philosopher condoned abortion generally or for personal convenience. Rather, each held a utilitarian view of the individual, born or unborn, seeing that individual as existing for the state. No rights granted to the individual were absolute. All rights—even the right to life—were subordinate to the welfare of the state (or the family, the religion or the race) and had to be sacrificed if the best interests of the state demanded it. Because territory was limited, one major concern of Greek city states was the problem of overpopulation and consequent poverty and weakness. This concern at least partially explains the philosophers' application of their utilitarian and subordinate view of the individual to the newborn or unborn, issuing in admonitions to expose or abort those that might be useless or damaging to the state.

Evidence for the positions of other Greek philosophical schools is slim. One important fact which is preserved is that the Stoics believed that the fetus is part of the mother and that life begins only with the fully developed infant's taking its first breath.[17] Given this viewpoint, one would expect the Stoics not to have opposed abortion, but if a first-century A.D. Stoic comment reflects earlier opinion, just the opposite was true. Musonius Rufus referred to abortion as "detrimental to the common good" and an act of impiety; he approved of the laws against it.[18] We know that Musonius and his predecessors supported large families, a fact which explains their opposition to abortion even though they believed the fetus is not a person. Although the Stoics differed from Plato and Aristotle, they all shared a common view of the welfare of the family and state—not the rights or life of the unborn—as the foremost consideration in the question of the propriety of abortion. Despite their antiabortion position, the Stoics' view of the beginning of human life, coupled with philosophical support for abortion, challenged Christian thinkers in later years.[19]

The later Stoics may have been influenced by the religious beliefs of the Orphics, who were the first Greeks to be concerned with the unborn's fate. This concern was prompted by an eschatology based on the idea that there is a normal cycle of life and death and a subsequent bodiless existence of the soul. People who die prematurely—such as those aborted—are doomed to an evil fate after death. This belief led to a condemnation of abortion, exposure and infanticide.[20]

Only one other Greek religious view of abortion is known. Several Greek inscriptions at public and private temples throughout the Mediterranean world mention birth, miscarriage and abortion as things which cause ritual, though not moral, impurity. After such events, a period of purification and abstinence from worship was required.[21] As in law and philosophy and probably also in medicine, no specific concern for the unborn is manifested.

The extent to which abortion was actually practiced in Greece is difficult to determine, but there are reasons to believe that it was not rare. The very fact of its being mentioned in a variety of contexts, the need to avoid overpopulation, and the frequency of infanticide and exposure (the latter with only rare condemnation) suggest that abortion was widely practiced. Though exposure may have been the preferred Greek method of controlling population quantity and quality, abortion was also useful.

The Roman Monarchy and Republic

Information about abortion in ancient Rome is only somewhat more extensive than that for ancient Greece. Although there are few explicit references to abortion during the Monarchy and most of the Republic, there is evidence that the practice increased over the centuries and by the first century B.C. was widespread.

According to Plutarch's first-century A.D. account of the laws enacted by Rome's namesake and legendary founder, Romulus, one just cause for a husband's divorcing his wife was her use of poisonous drugs.[22] Although various drugs were used for contraception and sterilization as well as abortion, it is likely that Plutarch was referring at least to abortion.[23] Whether Plutarch's report reflects ancient law or his own opinion cannot be determined with certainty, but in either case, the text reveals a typical

Roman view of abortion as an offense against the husband and father.[24]

The legal and moral climate of the Roman Republic was in fact determined by the power of the father, the *patria potestas*. The father, or *paterfamilias*, at first had nearly absolute power, all rights being his alone. His slaves, wife and children were all "taken in hand," *mancipia*, to him, and he had the power of life and death, *jus vitae necisque*, over them all. The *paterfamilias* could kill, mutilate and sell people like possessions.

Although his power was slightly weakened by custom and law, it continued without significant change until the time of the Empire. This power extended over both the newborn and the unborn. The earliest Roman law code, The Twelve Tables (ca 450 B.C.), permitted a father to expose any female infant he wished and any deformed baby of either sex.[25] In the early Republic, exposure was probably more common and accepted than abortion, but neither was ever punished as a crime per se. The Twelve Tables proposed social and political censure for husbands who ordered or permitted their wives to abort without good reason, but no fines or penalties were exacted from them, and those outside the family who might have been involved were unaffected by the law.[26]

In the revolutionary period of 145-30 B.C., Roman morals as well as economics were devastated. Murder and other crimes were commonplace, and increased freedom for women added to the incidence of divorce, adultery and abortion. The *Lex Cornelia* of 81 B.C. was enacted against assassins and poisoners. It is possible that this law applied also to abortion, either to the potential mothers or to those who supplied abortifacient drugs: the later Roman jurist Ulpian (ca A.D. 170-223) listed banishment as the appropriate application of *Lex Cornelia* to women who aborted.[27] On the other hand, Roman law never viewed the fetus as a human being but rather as part of the maternal viscera.[28] From this perspective, application of the *Lex Cornelia* to those who aided in abortion seems unlikely unless, since the law fo-

cused on harmful as well as on fatal drugs, the seller of abortifacient drugs might have been found guilty of harm not to the
fetus but to the woman.[29]

There is some evidence, then, that the late Republic enacted a
law to punish sellers of abortifacient drugs but not because they
caused abortions. Roman law did not consider the fetus a person, so there could be no law to protect rights which did not
exist.

The beginning of outspoken opposition to abortion, which
was continued by some later Romans, may be found in the greatest of Roman orators, Cicero (106-43 B.C.). In a speech given in
about 65 B.C., Cicero reported on a Milesian woman who had
aborted and was subsequently put to death. In what appears to
be his approval of this action and a condemnation of the moral
laxity of his day, Cicero calls for capital punishment for deliberate abortion. His apparent wish to enforce criminal penalties for
abortion is based on its injustice to the father, the family name,
the family's inheritance rights, the human race and the state.[30]
He makes no reference to harm to the mother or the fetus; Cicero
is reflecting a very Roman approach to abortion. But is this really
his opinion or is it merely the moral and legal rhetoric for which
he was famous and with which he almost certainly stretched the
truth throughout this entire speech? In the end, it makes no
difference, for he puts forth at least a *theoretical* Roman moralist
critique of the practice of abortion as it was known at the end of
the Republic.

When Octavian (later called Caesar Augustus) appeared on
the political scene, the Roman Republic was in disastrous moral
and economic straits. The practice of abortion, which had
reached an unprecedented height in the first century B.C., remained at a high rate throughout that century and the next. If
voices were raised against the abortion epidemic in the name of
the state, the father, or the pregnant woman, they went largely
unheeded. The widespread practice was inherited, and in some
cases perpetuated, by the Caesars.

The Roman Empire

Although explicit references to abortion are rare in the Greek period and in Rome before the Empire, both pagan and Christian writers attest to its universality during the Empire. Rich and poor, slave and free, young and old aborted themselves and were given abortions. Various efforts, pagan and Christian, were made to limit abortion, although no legislation making abortion itself a crime in the Roman Empire was enacted until the third century.

When Octavian was named Caesar Augustus in 27 B.C., he needed and wanted to build a strong state. In his opinion, a vital state necessitated strong families. Augustus therefore attempted to reform laws and morals, especially those concerning the family. He and his successors limited the *patria potestas* in order to give more state protection to the institution of the family. By law and by speech, Augustus tried to combat celibacy, childlessness, and family limiting by means of contraception, abortion or infanticide.[31] His edict concerning cutthroats and poisoners was probably applied to sellers of abortifacients,[32] and the *Lex Julia de maritandis ordinibus* of 18 B.C. and the *Lex Papia Poppaea* of A.D. 9 promoted childbearing rather than abortion and similar practices.[33] The Augustan reform, however, never forbade the act of abortion because Roman law adopted the Stoic view that the unborn is not human.[34] Thus the state became profamily but not fundamentally antiabortion.

Despite certain legal attempts by Augustus to restrain it, abortion flourished. Growing sensitivity to infanticide and exposure led to an increase in the less visible and therefore less offensive practice of abortion.[35] Great advances in medicine contributed to this phenomenon. Gynecology developed as a science. There were many woman physicians, some of whom wrote handbooks on abortion which were read by rich women and prostitutes.[36] Both mechanical and chemical contraception were practiced; when contraception failed, abortion could be performed in many ways. Reflecting on the widespread practice of abortion among the women of his day, Seneca (ca 3 B.C.-A.D. 65) lauded his own mother for not participating in unchastity, "the greatest evil of our time," and for never having "crushed the hope of children that were being nurtured in [her] body."[37] Indeed, abortion was to be found even in the highest places; both Suetonius and Juvenal refer to the emperor Domitian's (A.D. 51-96) affair with his niece Julia and one (probably not the first) resultant pregnancy which Domitian ordered terminated; the abortion caused the niece's death.[38]

Despite the continued popularity of abortion, it was not condoned by all Romans. There were literary, medical, philosophical, legal and religious condemnations. One of the chief witnesses to how common abortion was in the early Roman Empire was the popular Latin poet Ovid (43 B.C.-A.D. 17). His sometimes nonchalant mention of the practice indicates the mood of his time.[39] Although no propagator of strict morals himself, Ovid claimed that "the first one who thought of detaching from the womb the fetus forming in it deserved to die by her own weapons."[40] Using warfare as a metaphor, he describes abortion:

Of what avail to fair woman to rest free from the burdens of war, nor choose with shield in arm to march in the fierce array, if, free from peril of battle, she suffer wounds from weapons of her own, and arm her unforeseeing hands to her own undoing?

She who first plucked forth the tender life deserved to die in the warfare she began. Can it be that, to spare your bosom the reproach of lines, you would scatter the tragic sands of deadly combat?[41]

He found abortion unnatural and impious: "Where is the maternal sense? Where are the pious wishes of the fathers?"[42] Conscious of its inherent dangers, he reproached his own mistress for having had an abortion.[43]

Favorinus (ca A.D. 80-150) spoke of abortion as only one degree less criminal than the exposure of infants.[44] A severe condemnation came from the pen of the great satirist Juvenal (ca

A.D. 57/67-127) writing in about A.D. 116:

> Poor women... endure the perils of childbirth, and all the troubles of nursing to which their lot condemns them; but how often does a gilded bed contain a woman that is lying in it? So great is the skill, so powerful the drugs, of the abortionist, paid to murder mankind within the womb.[45]

Juvenal's comments—though undoubtedly somewhat hyperbolic and rhetorical—equate abortion with murder.

According to Soranos, the great physician of Trajan's reign (A.D. 98-117) who gave precision to gynecology, some of his contemporaries held that abortion was never proper.[46] Others, including himself, maintained that abortion was improper to conceal adultery or to maintain feminine beauty, but that it was permissible to save the woman's life.[47]

Philosophical condemnation of abortion came from the Stoics. The Stoics taught that life is to be lived in accord with nature and in resignation to the divine will. Their ethical concern was with what is right, not with what produces the greatest happiness or best results. In Musonius Rufus, Stoicism reached a zenith of idealistic ethics and humanitarian concern.[48] This first-century A.D. Stoic was held in high esteem in the ancient world by pagans and Christians alike, and even today he has been called "the Roman Socrates." His popularity was not unmixed with opposition, especially by some emperors and other government officials, for Musonius opposed both gladiator fights and war.[49]

In a series of five discourses on marriage, sex and the family, Musonius proposed two purposes for marriage in accord with nature: to create a bond of love and communion (koinōnia) between husband and wife and to bear children.[50] Sexual intercourse, however, is designed only for the latter purpose and never for "mere pleasure-seeking."[51] He advocated large families, opposing infanticide and abortion. He also supported the laws (of either Lycurgus or Augustus) which rewarded large families and forbade and punished abortion (the use of abortive drugs).[52]

The context of Musonius's brief reference to abortion indicates his rationale for opposing it. The text is found in *Discourse* 15, called "Should Every Child That Is Born Be Raised?" The whole thrust of his essay is that having many children is beautiful and right. Abortion is against the nature of sex and the logic of large families, which also provide men with more power and influence. Clearly he opposed abortion because it, like infanticide, reduces family size. Abortion (as one of several means of avoiding having many children) is, therefore, an offense against the gods, the family and nature, but not against the fetus. The Stoics continued to believe that life begins only at birth.

There are few non-Christian religious texts dealing with abortion. What remains is a handful of inscriptions describing the ritual impurity associated with abortion, similar to inscriptions of earlier centuries. No concern for the fetus is present in these inscriptions.[53]

Legal reaction to abortion also witnessed to its universality, but there is no indication that it had any effect in controlling abortion. As we have seen, there is no evidence for any legislation against abortion per se during the time of the Republic or the stormy transition period of Augustus. Neither is there any evidence for such legislation during the first two centuries of the Empire.[54] But Justinian's *Digest* preserves fragments from the very late second and third centuries.

The first Roman action against abortion as a crime in itself was a rescript enacted by the emperor Septimus Severus (reigned A.D. 193-211) and continued by his successor Antoninus Caracalla (reigned A.D. 211-217). Abortion was classified among the *crimina extraordinaria*, crimes punished arbitrarily, outside the formulary system and without fixed penalty. The rescript prescribed exile of an unspecified (but not permanent) length for a wife who procured an abortion, because "it might appear scandalous that she should be able to deprive her husband of children without being punished."[55] The concern of the rescript was only with the husband's rights and the wife's duties, and not at

all with the "rights" of the fetus or the woman. Ulpian recorded
that such a punishment was given also as an application of Caesar Augustus's *Lex Cornelia* (concerning assassins and poisoners)
to women found guilty of abortion.[56] Similarly, the jurist Try-
phonius referred to Cicero's record in *Pro Cluentio* of a woman
condemned to death for abortion; he recommended instead the
exile pronounced by "our very excellent emperors."[57] Tryphoni-
us applied this penalty specifically to a woman who aborted after
a divorce in order not to give a child to the former husband
whom she hated. This Roman's concern was apparently neither
for the child nor for the mother, but also only for the father's
rights.

The most comprehensive Roman legal pronouncement was recorded by the respected third-century jurist Paulus. In his *Sen-
tentiarum*, a compendium of undisputed legal principles, Paulus
wrote:

> Because the thing is a bad example, lower-class people who
> give a drink to cause an abortion or to excite passion (although
> they don't do it deceitfully), are to be condemned to the
> mines, and more distinguished persons to be relegated to an
> island and deprived of a part of their wealth. If by this drink a
> woman or a man has died, they are condemned to capital
> punishment.[58]

This condemnation of abortion by means of drugs saw it not as
murder, unless death to the woman occurred, but as a bad example. The guilty party in either case, according to Paulus, was the
aide. Under this code and the contemporary interpretation of the
Lex Cornelia, by no later than the third century A.D. dealers in
abortifacient drugs worked at some risk of legal punishment.[59]
To what extent these laws were enforced, however, must remain
a question.

According to the *Digest*, by the third century A.D. Roman law
considered abortion an offense against the father and a bad
example.[60] Danger to the mother and disregard for the rights of
future citizens may also have been motives for legal condemna-

tion.[61] However, as far as we can ascertain from historical records, the pagan Roman Empire prescribed no punishment for abortion with the consent of the father unless poisons were used or the mother died.[62] Furthermore, concern for the unborn was minimal or nonexistent. The underlying legal principles in these attitudes were undoubtedly the continued though weakened importance of the *paterfamilias*, the traditional condemnation of poisons, the idea of a crime as fundamentally an offense against the state and, above all, the view that the fetus is not a human being—a Stoic notion given legal status according to the important Roman jurist Papinian (A.D. 140-212).[63] That the fetus is not a person was fundamental to Roman law.[64] Even when born, the child was valued primarily not for itself but for its usefulness to the father, the family and especially the state, as a citizen "born for the state."[65]

Although the Roman Empire continued to exist into the late fifth century, a special situation arose with the advent of Constantine (in 306) and his "Christian" empire. The abortion discussion of that age is treated in chapter five.

3
THE JEWISH WORLD

AN EXCEPTION TO THE FREQUENT PRACTICE of abortion in antiquity was found among the Jews. Despite the absence of a specific condemnation or prohibition of abortion in their Scriptures, extensive research has discovered no mention of a nontherapeutic Jewish abortion in any texts of the Hebrew Bible or of other Jewish literature through A.D. 500.[1] Only a few prohibitions of abortion have been preserved in Jewish literature from about 150 B.C. Furthermore, the Talmud, the multivolume collection of centuries of Jewish rabbinic opinion which was assembled about A.D. 500, contains many discussions of miscarriage and therapeutic abortion but only one definite reference to deliberate, unnecessary abortion, and that is almost certainly directed to non-Jews. It was a given of Jewish thought and life that abortion, like exposure, was unacceptable, and this was well known in the ancient world. From 300 B.C. through the era of the Talmud, both pagans (such as Hecataeus of Abdera in Egypt and the Roman historian Tacitus) and Jews testify to the Jews' love for and religious duty of begetting children.[2] Tacitus notes that this led to their rejection of exposure; it was also one of their reasons for rejecting abortion. Though rare cases of abortion may have occurred in Judaism, the witness of antiquity is that Jews, unlike pagans, did not practice deliberate abortion.

Although the Jews did not practice abortion, they did discuss the fetus and its death in a variety of contexts. Behind each of these discussions is assumed a basic Jewish orientation to life: first, the duty and desire to populate the earth and ensure both Jewish survival and the divine presence; second, a deep sense of the sanctity of life as God's creation, a respect extending in various ways to life in all its manifestations and stages; and, finally, a profound horror of blood and bloodshed.[3] These themes undergird the entire Jewish approach to abortion.

Despite this fundamentally unified outlook, the Jews approached the subject of the fetus and its death in several different ways. Scholars generally hold that there were two major schools of Jewish thought about abortion, the Alexandrian and the majority Palestinian, as well as a minor school, the minority Palestinian.[4] Within each school there were both legal and ethical pronouncements. We will approach the material according to the three schools.

The Alexandrian School

The Alexandrian school of Jewish thought was influenced both by Greek philosophical ideas present in Alexandria and by the actual pagan practice of abortion.[5] When the translators of the Septuagint (the Greek Old Testament) came to the Hebrew text of Exodus 21:22-25, it read as follows (my translation):

> If men strive together and strike a pregnant woman so that her child comes out of her, but there is no harm, [the guilty one] will surely be fined according to what the woman's husband

demands of him, and he will pay according to the judges'
decision. But if there is harm, then you must give life for life,
eye for eye, tooth for tooth.

This text can be understood to mean "harm" to the woman or to
the fetus. Whether correctly or not, in Palestine the question of
"harm" was understood to refer not to the fetus but only to the
woman. Aware of the philosophical debate between Plato, who
said life begins at conception, and the Stoics, who said life begins at birth, and aware also of the Aristotelian distinction between the formed and the unformed fetus, the Septuagint translators rendered the Hebrew word '*ason* ("harm") as "form." The
phrase "there is no harm" became "there is no form." The result
was as follows:

> If two men fight and they strike a woman who is pregnant,
> and her child comes out while not yet fully formed, the one
> liable to punishment will be fined; whatever the woman's
> husband imposes, he will give as is fitting. But if it is fully
> formed, he will give life for life.[6]

The change of "harm" to "form" makes the penalty apply explicitly to injuring the fetus, not the woman. This translation expresses a prior belief about the fetus which is basically Aristotelian and is a *via media* between Stoics and Platonists.[7] The fetus
is not a person until fully formed (probably at forty days, possibly eighty for females). The destruction of the fully formed fetus
is punished not just by fine, as in the then-current interpretation
of the Hebrew text, but by death. The Septuagint text of Exodus
21, then, reflects Alexandrian Jewish philosophical opinion on
the nature of the fetus and legal opinion on the penalties for accidental abortion. It may also reflect the general Alexandrian response to the practice of deliberate abortion.[8]

Philo of Alexandria (25 B.C.-A.D. 41) adapts the Septuagint
version of Exodus 21 still further. In his *Special Laws*, which is
an exposition of the Ten Commandments and other Jewish laws,
Philo includes the following discussion under his section on the
commandment "Thou shalt not kill":

If a man comes to blows with a pregnant woman and strikes her on the belly and she miscarries, then, if the result of the miscarriage is unshaped and undeveloped, he must be fined both for the outrage and for obstructing the artist Nature in her creative work of bringing into life the fairest of living creatures, man. But, if the offspring is already shaped and all the limbs have their proper qualities and places in the system, he must die, for that which answers to this description is a human being, which he has destroyed in the laboratory of Nature who judges that the hour has not yet come for bringing it out into the light, like a statue lying in a studio requiring nothing more than to be conveyed outside and released from confinement.[9]

Philo changes the struggle between two men, resulting in accidental injury to a fetus, into one man's deliberate attack on a pregnant woman. He maintains the Septuagint's distinction between the unformed and formed fetus and, consequently, between the penalties of a fine and death. However, he shifts the emphasis of the text from these legal distinctions to the judgment that the one who harms the unformed fetus is guilty of an outrage against Nature and that the one who harms the formed fetus is guilty of the murder of a human being and is thus deserving of death.

Philo's comparison of the formed fetus to a sculpture in the studio is his parabolic way of expressing an impassioned moral conviction, one that goes beyond the evil of attacking pregnant women. He is also challenging the justification of abortion by legal, medical and philosophical authorities who, he declares, claim that "the child while still adhering to the womb below the belly is part of its future mother."[10] His overriding concern is not with the father (is he the attacker?), as in Roman law, but with the child. He sees the problem fundamentally as a moral issue related not only to Exodus 21 but, more important, to the commandment against murder. This connection between abortion and murder was also made by early Christian writers, who further developed the idea.

While the translators of the Septuagint and the philosopher Philo distinguished the nonhuman from the human fetus (recommending appropriate penalties for the death of each), this legal concern should not be seen as the primary aim of these writers or of Alexandrian Judaism generally. Rather, their fundamental concern is the serious immorality of killing *any* unborn, especially when the killing is deliberately executed. This emphasis is strikingly reflected in two Alexandrian writings which have no legal concerns at all. The first, known as the *Sentences of Pseudo-Phocylides*, is a collection of ethical maxims about conduct in daily life. It was written probably between 50 B.C. and A.D. 50 in the tradition of ancient wisdom literature. In the section on sexuality, marriage and the family, the author writes:

A woman should not destroy the unborn babe in her belly, nor after its birth throw it before the dogs and the vultures as a prey.[11]

In this ethical context the author does not make fine legal distinctions, even if he holds them. Instead, his concern is ethical and practical; he wishes to prevent the pagan practices of abortion and exposure from infiltrating the Jewish community. Besides his obvious concern for the child, the writer is—like all Jews and like the Stoics who influenced him—extremely favorable to procreation.[12]

A similar blanket condemnation of abortion is found in a contemporary work of a different sort, the *Sibylline Oracles*. The *Oracles* are an example of first- and second-century B.C. apocalyptic literature. The section of book 2 on the punishment of the wicked includes women who abort or expose their children:

Having burdens in the womb [they]
Produce abortions; and their offspring cast
Unlawfully away . . .[13]

These women will suffer the wrath of God along with sorcerers (who dispense, among other things, abortifacients). Also included in his wrath are adulterers, thieves, the impure, and oppressors of the poor and of widows.[14] Again, the writer has no

interest in legal fine points but is concerned only with the fundamental immorality of abortion.

In summary, the Alexandrian Jewish position viewed abortion as immoral and punishable. In ethical contexts it stressed
the immorality of abortion without concerning itself with legal
and technical questions about the fetus, while in more legal
contexts it discussed the nature of the act and its appropriate
penalty. However, even in legal contexts the Alexandrian school,
as represented by Philo, was more concerned with the immorality of deliberate abortion than with legal penalties.

The Palestinian Schools

We find the bulk of Palestinian opinion on our subject in the
Mishnah, the Talmud and the writings of Josephus. The Mishnah, compiled by Rabbi Judah (ca 135-ca 220), includes topically
arranged sections ("tractates") embodying several centuries of
rabbinic legal pronouncements. The Talmud, compiled about
A.D. 500, contains the Mishnah plus "Gemara," or later rabbinic
comments upon the material found in the Mishnah. Josephus
(A.D. ca 37-ca 100) was a famous historian, defender of the Jewish faith and critic of pagan society.

Palestinian discussion of the fetus and its death revolved
around four key issues: the development of the fetus, its religious and legal status, accidental or necessary feticide, and deliberate feticide. In Palestine, unlike Alexandria, Jewish concern
with abortion was almost totally with the problem of the legal
and cultic status of the fetus, especially in miscarriages and certain necessary (and usually late) abortions. Abortion in the early
stages of pregnancy, "on demand" or as a means of birth control,
"is very likely not even contemplated in the Mishnaic law."[15]
This is important to realize in reading the Talmud and the Mishnah, since most English editions of these works use the word
abortion as a synonym for miscarriage or miscarried fetus.

It is frequently said that there was basically one Palestinian
perspective on abortion, a perspective which stood in contrast

to the Alexandrian view. A closer examination of the evidence, however, suggests that there were two significant schools of rabbinic thought on the subject, the majority opinion and a strong, vocal minority opinion. An examination of the debate shows the differences between these views.

As in Alexandria and elsewhere in the ancient world, in Palestine there was debate on the time of a person's ensoulment and formation. Though the debate may have come into Judaism directly from the pagan world, it was further stimulated by Old Testament creation texts (for example, Gen 1:27; 2:7; 2:19) which use words like *soul* and especially *form*.[16]

The time of ensoulment was held to be either at birth, formation or conception. The compiler of the Mishnah, Rabbi Judah, is reported to have changed his mind on the time of ensoulment during a conversation with one Antonius:

> Antonius also said to Rabbi, "When is the soul placed in man; as soon as it is decreed [that the sperm shall be male or female], or when [the embryo] is actually formed?" He replied, "From the moment of formation." He objected: "Can a piece of meat be unsalted for three days without becoming putrid? But it must be from the moment that [God] decrees its destiny." Rabbi said; "This thing Antonius taught me, and Scripture supports him, for it is written, *And thy decree hath preserved my spirit* [i.e., my soul].[17]

Similarly, there was discussion about the time at which a Jew could enter the future world. Was it necessary to have passed conception, birth, circumcision or the time of one's first words?[18] These speculative debates about ensoulment and immortality, however, did not significantly affect the Jewish views on the death of a fetus.[19]

The issue of formation, on the other hand, did affect Jewish laws concerning a woman's postpartum uncleanness. Attempts were made to prove from Scripture that males were formed at forty days and females at eighty, but most rabbis believed that formation of both sexes took place at forty days.[20] Beyond this general consensus, rabbis were divided on the significance of formation. Although a minority held that the miscarriage of an unformed fetus was a "valid birth requiring purification of the mother," the majority opinion was that the miscarried fetus had to be fully formed for the birth to be considered valid:

> The Sages say: What is not of the form of man is not account-
> ed [human] young. If the abortion was a foetus filled with
> water or filled with blood or filled with variegated matter,
> she need not take thought for it as for [human] young; but if
> its [human] parts were fashioned, she must continue [unclean
> the number of days prescribed] both for a male and for a
> female.[21]

This does not mean, however, that the Jews' concern with miscarriage was that it might be the death of a person, although they called the fetus "human" young. Rather, their primary concern was the cultic issue of cleanness or uncleanness due to the blood of childbirth.[22] That the primary concern was cultic is confirmed by the majority view on Caesarean sections. These were not valid births and did not make a woman's house unclean, because the blood of birth did not pass through the area where conception took place.[23]

Even if human life was not the issue in Palestinian Jewish laws on miscarriage, did the Jews consider the fetus to be human life? Again, there was a majority position and a minority view expressed in legal contexts. The majority view was grounded in the Hebrew text of Exodus 21, which, as we have seen, differs significantly from the Greek Septuagint. The Hebrew text bears repeating:

> If men strive together and strike a pregnant woman, so that
> her child comes out of her, but there is no harm, [the guilty
> one] will surely be fined according to what the woman's hus-
> band demands of him, and he will pay according to the
> judges' decision. But if there is harm, then you must give life
> for life, eye for eye, tooth for tooth.

The situation described is an accidental miscarriage, not a de-

liberate (as in Philo) or even near-deliberate (as in the Septuagint) attack. In this text the word '*ason*, "harm," was understood
by the rabbis to refer to the death of the woman; the principle of
"life for life" was therefore applied only to her death, not to the
miscarriage, for which only a fine was to be exacted. The passage
was adopted also by Josephus in his *Antiquities*, about A.D. 94:

> He that kicketh a woman with child, if the woman miscarry,
> shall be fined by the judges for having, by the destruction of
> the fruit of her womb, diminished the population, and a fur-
> ther sum shall be presented by him to the woman's husband.
> If she die of the blow, he also shall die, the law claiming as its
> due the sacrifice of life for life.[24]

Here Josephus recognizes the damaging effects of the loss of a
fetus: the harm to the woman, her husband and society. His Palestinian perspective, however, leads him not to consider the
damage to the fetus itself but rather to follow the Hebrew text's
legal structure even in a situation which appears less accidental
than the original situation in Exodus 21.

  This Exodus passage led the majority of the rabbis to assert
that the fetus does not have the legal status of a person. Indeed,
as in Roman law, they taught that the fetus is a part of the mother:

> The embryo is part [literally, "a thigh"] of its mother. [The]
> embryo [is regarded] as part of the mother, . . . one of her own
> limbs.

Describing a pregnant woman, the rabbis say:

> There was originally one body and now also there is one body.

Since the fetus has no legal existence as an independent being, it
has no legal rights:

> A babe who is one day old inherits and transmits... but not
> an embryo![25]

In the case of the fetus, Roman and Hebrew laws were identical.

  From the majority perspective, therefore, certain abortions
are permissible and even mandatory. In the case of mortal danger to the mother, the fetus is considered an aggressor and must
be aborted unless more than half its head or half its body (if it

is in the breech position) has been born:

> If a woman was in hard travail, the child must be cut up while it is in the womb and brought out member by member, since the life of the mother has priority over the life of the child; but if the greater part of it was already born, it may not be touched, since the claim of one life cannot override the claim of another life.[26]

It is important to notice that the Mishnah does not deny the presence of life, in some sense, in the fetus. Rather, the general principle is to save existing, "born" persons. The mother's life takes precedence over that of the fetus.[27]

According to the majority opinion, the fetus has no "juridical personality." This view of the fetus as an appendage of the mother must be understood solely as a legal evaluation enabling the rabbis to understand and judge the daily affairs of women involved in accidental or therapeutic abortions. In the words of a Jewish scholar:

> Germane as all of the above information might seem to the question of abortion, it could hardly be sufficient for determining the morality of such action. It merely defines the legal status of the foetus.[28]

When the issue of deliberate abortion arises, these rabbis have very little or nothing to say. This fact can be explained partially by the extreme rarity of abortion in Judaism. We cannot know, then, how these rabbis viewed deliberate abortion from a legal perspective (if they considered it at all). However, we can determine their basic ethical attitude toward abortion.

Despite legal indifference to the fetus, the Talmud shows an appreciation for the work of the Creator in forming the unborn life:

> Our rabbis taught: There are three partners in man, the Holy One, blessed be He, his father and his mother. . . .
>
> What is the purport of the Scriptural text, *I will give thanks unto thee, for I am fearfully and wonderfully made?* . . . If a dyer puts different ingredients into a boiler they all unite into one

colour, whereas the Holy One, blessed be He, fashions the embryo in a woman's bowels in a manner [such] that each develops in its own natural way.[29]

The Talmud also promotes a sense of duty to propagate the Jewish people and thus preserve the divine presence. The one who will not propagate is like one who "sheds blood and diminishes the Divine Image" and "causes the Divine Presence to depart from Israel."[30] It is unlikely that such perspectives could peacefully coexist with permissive views of deliberate abortion.

In his discussion of accidental feticide, as we have seen, Josephus expresses the majority Palestinian view which does not give the fetus legal status. Nevertheless, in his later apology for Judaism, *Against Apion*, Josephus writes:

The Law orders all the offspring to be brought up, and forbids women either to cause abortion or to make away with the foetus; a woman convicted of this is regarded as an infanticide, because she destroys a soul and diminishes the race.[31]

Several difficulties arise from this text. To what law does Josephus refer? Does he assume a distinction between the formed and the unformed fetus? One point, however, is clear: despite his legal opinion that the fetus is not a person, when Josephus speaks from an ethical perspective, he calls deliberate abortion murder. The "Law," then, may well be the Ten Commandments, particularly "Thou shalt not kill." Opposition to abortion in this passage stems not only from concern for the Jewish people and law but also from respect for the fetus as an individual endowed with a soul. Although it is likely that Josephus's contact with the non-Jewish world motivated his addressing the issue of deliberate abortion, it nevertheless seems safe to assume that his contemporary Palestinian rabbis shared this perspective. The example of Josephus proves that holding a permissive legal view of abortion in certain circumstances does not rule out forcefully condemning deliberate abortion as immoral and even as murder.

The minority Palestinian view asserted that the fetus is legally

a person with some measure of personal and legal rights. The unborn has spiritual life, rationality and the ability to praise God.
A dead fetus in the womb is a dead person, even, according to
some, rendering the mother and the house unclean.[32] (Despite
this view of the fetus as a person, the minority view did permit
therapeutic abortion.[33]) The biblical basis for this view of the
unborn's personhood was found in Genesis 9:6, which Rabbi
Ishmael and others read in this way:

> Whoso sheddeth the blood of man within [another] man, shall
> his blood be shed.

They understood "man within man" to mean the fetus in the
mother; the fetus, in this interpretation, is a person.

What motivated this minority view? Their evaluation of the
fetus as an independent being seems to have been based on her-
meneutical differences with the majority, who interpreted
"within man" to mean "within the murderer":

> Whoso sheddeth the blood of man, within [that] man [him-
> self] shall his blood be shed.

Since this Genesis text is pre-Sinai and hence pre-Israel, both
sides understood the verse to prescribe capital punishment for
non-Jews. The minority view interpreted it to prescribe the
death penalty for abortion; the majority thought it prescribed
strangulation as the means of capital punishment for murderers.[34] Perhaps the minority view was influenced by Greek philosophical debate about the fetus. In any event, there is no evidence that the minority ever applied the death penalty in cases
where Jewish women miscarried, and, as we have seen, there is
no discussion of deliberate Jewish abortions. The minority's
recommendation of the death penalty to non-Jews for abortion,
obviously beyond their power to enforce, can best be understood as exegesis motivated by horror at the pagan practice of
abortion.[35]

The Two Jewish Views

It is generally accepted that two Jewish views on abortion existed, the Alexandrian and the Palestinian. According to most scholars, the strict Alexandrian view required punishment for damage to a fetus according to its stage of development, whereas the more lenient Palestinian view, holding that the fetus was not a person, required punishment only for harm to the mother.[36] This analysis, though prevalent, is not entirely accurate.

In the first place, both Alexandrian and Palestinian schools discussed the personhood of the fetus from a legal, not an ethical, standpoint. Differing legal interpretations may or may not represent differing moral judgments. Second, both schools confined their discussion to accidental or therapeutic abortions. Neither considered the possibility of induced abortion for less than life-threatening reasons. Third, the Palestinian view was not itself unified. The minority view, which had a sizable following, joined with the Alexandrians in granting legal personhood to the fetus. Fourth, and most important, Jews of both regions united on the subject of deliberate abortion. Alexandrians and Palestinians of both the majority and the minority legal opinions condemned deliberate abortion as disrespect for life and as bloodshed.

In the Jewish mind a clear distinction was continually maintained between accidental/therapeutic and deliberate abortions. The former case was an issue open to debate; the latter, a settled matter. Clearly the division in Judaism was not between a strict (Alexandrian) and a lenient (Palestinian) approach to *deliberate* abortion. The division of opinion was rather over the severity of the penalty to be exacted in cases of *accidental* or *therapeutic* abortion. This interpretation alone reconciles the otherwise contradictory statements of Josephus discussed above.

The Jewish abhorrence of deliberate bloodshed and its respect for life, including that of the unborn, formed a natural foundation for the Christian writings on abortion.

4
CHRISTIAN BEGINNINGS: THE FIRST THREE CENTURIES

SO FAR WE HAVE DESCRIBED REASONS for and means of abortion in antiquity and have outlined pagan and Jewish opinion and practice. It was within this historical situation that Christianity arose and had to face the theological, ethical and very human issue of abortion.

Writers of the first three Christian centuries laid the theological and literary foundation for all subsequent early Christian writing on abortion. We will see that three important themes emerged during these centuries: the fetus is the creation of God; abortion is murder; and the judgment of God falls on those guilty of abortion. A theological question also arose. Is the fetus a human life from the time of conception? These themes were expressed in a variety of literary contexts: the tradition of "two ways," the commandment against murder, apocalyptic visions of hell, interpretations of biblical texts, apologies for Christian behavior, discussions of the origin of the soul, and reflections on the actual practice of abortion in specific cases. These issues and their contexts were developed further by later writers.

The New Testament

Although the New Testament makes no specific reference to abortion, the association of the use of drugs *(pharmakeia)* with abortion in pagan and later Christian writings suggests that there may be an implicit reference to abortion in such texts as Galatians 5:20 and Revelation 9:21, 18:23, 21:8 and 22:15, where words of the same group are used.[1] This suggestion is by no means far-fetched. The word *pharmakeia* (and its cognates) can be a neutral, generic term for the use of drugs, but more often it has the negative connotation of drugs and potions supplied by a sorcerer or magician. It is also used to refer to poisons and mind-disturbing drugs.[2] In Soranos's *Gynecology*, it refers specifically to the use of one type of evil drug, the abortifacient.[3] The word *pharmakeia* itself, then, can mean the use of drugs, evil or magical drugs themselves, or a specific evil drug such as a poison or an abortifacient.

The contexts of the New Testament references to *pharmakeia* demand an understanding of the word in a negative sense. Vice lists and apocalyptic passages like those of Galatians and Revelation became standard literary settings in the early church for the denunciation of moral evils. Moreover, noncanonical condemnation of abortion before A.D. 125 is found in connection with the same related sins of fornication and murder which appear in the texts of Galatians and Revelation where *pharmakeia* is used. Thus, while a conclusive affirmation of explicit New Testament condemnation of abortion is impossible, the word *pharmakeia* and the contexts in which it is found suggest that Galatians and Revelation implicitly reject at least one major means of abortion in their rejection of magic, drugs and poisons.[4]

The Earliest Discussions

The earliest specific written references to abortion are those in the *Didache* and the *Epistle of Barnabas*. The *Didache* combines a code of Christian morality with a manual of church life and order, while the *Epistle of Barnabas* is a more theological tract on Christian life and thought. While both of these probably date from the early second century, they most likely drew on Christian sources which had their origins in the late first century.[5]

Both these writings also contain a section based on a Jewish oral and written tradition known as the "Two Ways." This tradition contrasts the two ways of Life or Light and Death or Darkness. Athanasius notes that it was used extensively in the early church, either as a separate document or as part of the *Didache*, especially for the training of catechumens and new converts.[6]

The *Didache* maintains that there is a "great difference" between these two ways.[7] In an exposition of the second great commandment ("Love your neighbor as yourself") as part of the Way of Life, the author makes a list of "thou shalt not" statements obviously modeled on, and in part quoting, the Decalogue of the Septuagint. The list of prohibitions includes murder, adultery, sodomy, fornication, theft, the use of magic and philters, infanticide and abortion.[8] Literally, it declares: "Thou shalt not murder a child by abortion/destruction."[9] Similarly, the *Epistle of Barnabas*, in its practical section on the Way of Light, repeats exactly the same words in a list of "thou shalt (not)" statements including, just before the abortion prohibition, "Thou shalt love thy neighbor more than thy own life."[10] The fetus is seen, not as a part of its mother, but as a neighbor. Abortion is rejected as contrary to other-centered neighbor love.[11]

On the other hand, the Way of Death, according to the *Didache*, is full of cursing, murders, adulteries, idolatries, robberies and hypocrisies. It is also filled with people who are "murderers of children,"[12] an echo of the prohibition against abortion (though it may also refer to infanticide), and "corrupters of God's creatures,"[13] which a third-century Latin version renders *abortu-*

antes,reflecting knowledge of the use of the Greek term *phtho-reus* for abortionists.[14] The *Epistle of Barnabas* uses the same two phrases in its description of the "way of the Black one," the way of "death eternal with punishment."[15] In both writings the immediate context includes both personal vices and more socially oriented evils such as turning away the needy and oppressing the afflicted.

The significance of these two writings lies both in their firm position on abortion as murder and in their development of an ethical context within which abortion should be viewed. "Thou shalt not abort" becomes a subcommandment of the commandment not to murder. It has a status, in this document, almost on a par with the Decalogue itself. The commandment form is a succinct and unqualified continuation of the Jewish condemnation of deliberate abortion. There is no formed/unformed distinction, no elaboration.[16] Abortion is presented also as an offense against humanity, a defiance of the second great commandment—"Love thy neighbor"—which the *Epistle of Barnabas* has expanded to say "more than thyself." Furthermore, abortion is depicted not only as a sin like sexual immorality, but as an evil no less severe and social in scope than oppression of the poor and needy and no less dishonorable than the use of poisons.

The *Didache* and the *Epistle of Barnabas* were extremely important in two other respects. First, the widespread use of their "Two Ways" teachings among early Christians assured the disseminating of their position on abortion. Second, later writings appropriated the murder definition, the commandment form, the elevation of the status of the fetus and the context of personal and social evils found in these two early works.

Contemporary with or just after these earliest documents was the *Apocalypse of Peter*, the most important of the noncanonical apocalypses. It was held in great esteem by the early church and was given canonical status by Clement of Alexandria and by the oldest list of the New Testament canon, the *Muratorian Fragment*, although it was rejected from the canon in the fourth century.[17]

Probably under the influence of oriental and Orphic-Pythagorean eschatology, the author of this apocalypse paints a graphic portrait of hell's population, which includes this scene:

> And near that place I saw another gorge in which the discharge and excrement of the tortured ran down and became like a lake. And there sat women, and the discharge came up to their throats; and opposite them sat many children, who were born prematurely, weeping. And from them went forth rays of fire and smote the women on the eyes. And these were those who produced children outside marriage and who procured abortions.[18]

The context of this passage, similar to *Barnabas*, includes punishments for blasphemers, murderers, the rich who trusted in riches and neglected orphans and widows, usurers, homosexuals and idolaters.[19]

Another text tradition of this apocalypse, longer than the fragmentary one above, provides for the damnation of both husbands and wives guilty of abortion and for the salvation of the aborted infants:

> And the children shall be given to the [caretaking, protecting] angel Temlakos. And those who slew them will be tortured for ever, for God wills it to be so.[20]

These texts are important for their powerful presentation of the destiny of aborters and the aborted. It is evident that this picture is drawn, even with apocalyptic imagination, from deep ethical and emotional convictions. Especially gripping is the vision of the infants' vengeance on their mothers. Whatever judgment on that idea is made, the theological basis for the entire text must be seen as an understanding of abortion as the culpable murder of a human being. Unborn children are viewed as living beings destined for immortality, and both men and women responsible for aborting them are guilty and worthy of eternal punishment. Methodius of Olympus and Clement of Alexandria were later inspired by this apocalyptic perspective.

Clement of Alexandria (ca 150-ca 215), in his *Prophetic Ec-*

logues, a commentary on earlier Christian writings, quotes the *Apocalypse of Peter* with approval, noting again that both exposed and aborted children will be delivered to safety by a caretaking angel but that the parents will suffer punishment because of their sins.[21]

In his *Prophetic Eclogues,* Clement also quotes an anonymous writer of the mid second century, perhaps a Christian Platonist, who argues that the fetus has a soul and is a living person.[22] His argument is based on the unusual idea that angels place the soul in the womb at the time of conception and the new embryo has a soul immediately.[23] The main significance of this text, however, is not in its philosophical and theological speculation but in its connection of questions about the life of the fetus to the New Testament. Clement records that this writer's proofs that the embryo is alive are the references in Luke 1 to John the Baptist and Jesus in their mothers' wombs. He makes particular use of Luke 1:41: "And when Elizabeth heard Mary's greeting, the baby leaped in her womb." Though the writer focuses on the Baptist and does not even mention abortion, he laid the groundwork for subsequent theological links between abortion and the Incarnation.[24]

In his own writings Clement brought both theology and ethics face to face with contemporary pagan society. In *The Tutor (Paedagogus),* written about 190-200, Clement addresses Christians concerning the goal of virtue to which the Logos, their tutor, could bring them.[25] In book 2, he pictures Alexandrian life in detail in order to warn Christians not to participate in all its luxury and vice and to provide them with a substitute moral code, calling them to extend the Christian spirit throughout the city. In the context of Christian marriage, the goal of which in Clement's opinion is procreation, he writes:

> Our whole life can go on in observation of the laws of nature, if we gain dominion over our desires from the beginning and if we do not kill, by various means of a perverse art, the human offspring, born according to the designs of divine providence;

for these women who, in order to hide their immorality, use abortive drugs which expel the matter completely dead, abort at the same time their human feelings.[26]

Clement continues the main themes of the Christian community: abortion is killing human life that is under God's care, design and providence. That he considered the unborn to be a human being is clear from the clause "if we do not kill *(kteinō)*" and is also implicit elsewhere in his thoughts on childbirth and the immortality of the soul.[27] Clement was greatly influenced by the Stoics, but his concern for the child itself goes beyond the Stoic concern for doing what is right and in accord with nature. Clement's own personal and sensitive contribution to the Christian position can be seen in his last clause, where he speaks of the aborting of human feeling *(philanthrōpia)*.

The Apologists

In the ancient world, the new Christian faith had two unavoidable tasks: self-definition and self-defense. Though these two needs were intimately intertwined, the writers we have just examined were concerned principally with self-definition. There was also a need for self-defense, for giving an explanation of and justification for Christian beliefs and practices. As the Christian faith encountered the world around it, there were natural tensions and conflicts due both to real differences and to mutual misunderstandings. The group of Fathers known as the Apologists arose to answer the pagan criticisms of their religion.

Athenagoras (mid to late second century), the ablest of the Greek apologists for Christianity, addressed the emperor Marcus Aurelius and his son Lucius Aurelius Commodus in 177. Athenagoras was concerned to answer three frequent charges made against Christianity—atheism, incest and cannibalism—and thus to uphold Christian belief and moral standards. To the charge of cannibalism, stemming from a misunderstanding of the Eucharist, Athenagoras responded that cannibalism implied murder and that Christians would not even *watch* a murder (for example, a gladiator fight), much less perform one. His defense continues:

> What reason would we have to commit murder when we say that women who induce abortions are murderers, and will have to give account of it to God? For the same person would not regard the fetus in the womb as a living thing and therefore an object of God's care [and then kill it]. . . . But we are altogether consistent in our conduct. We obey reason and do not override it. [28]

Athenagoras claims to represent the common, accepted Christian position; if it were not the accepted practice, his argument would lose all its force. The three important elements in the Christian position appear already in explicit form in this late second-century document: (1) abortion is considered murder; (2) the guilty must give account to God (a milder form of the apocalyptic imagery); (3) the fetus is a living being, the object of God's care. Athenagoras's contribution is to set the issue of abortion in an argument for Christian practice based on the Christian view of the sanctity of life. He writes that Christians have renounced murder in all its forms—mentioning the common Roman practices of gladiator contests, animal fights, exposure and abortion—in order to avoid becoming polluted and defiled. It is this absolute abhorrence of bloodshed in any form which drives them away from even looking at practices such as gladiator fights and criminal executions. This view stood in stark contrast to the prevailing Roman lifestyle.

The most eloquent apologist in the West was Tertullian (ca 160-ca 240), who ranks second only to Augustine for his Latin contributions to the church. His most important work is the *Apology*, written in 197 and directed to governors of Roman provinces and to the emperor Septimus Severus. Like Athenagoras in the East, Tertullian sought to defend Christianity against charges of immorality, atheism and even treason. In refuting accusations of secret crimes (chapters 7-9), he dismisses as a rumor the charge that "we are accused of observing a holy rite in which we kill a little child and then eat it."[29] Later, to strengthen his case, he adds:

> That I may refute more thoroughly these charges, I will show that in part openly, in part secretly, practices prevail among you which have led you perhaps to credit similar things about us.[30]

After citing mythological and historical cases of child sacrifice and exposure in the Greco-Roman world, Tertullian claims:

> In our case, murder being once for all forbidden, we may not destroy even the foetus in the womb, while as yet the human being derives blood from other parts of the body for its sustenance. To hinder a birth is merely a speedier man-killing; nor does it matter whether you take away a life that is born, or destroy one that is coming to the birth. That is a man which is going to be one; you have the fruit already in the seed.[31]

His comparison of the seed and the fruit conveys with imagination the universal Christian concern for life. It also has a parallel, probably independent but coming from the same ethical roots, in Philo's comparison of the embryo to a statue ready to be removed from the artist's studio.[32]

Tertullian reveals that the basis of the early Christian position on abortion was the commandment not to murder. Like earlier Christian writers, he considers the fetus a human being, though still dependent on the mother. Speaking for the Christian community, he consequently condemns abortion as "speedier" homicide. For Tertullian, dependence on the mother did not mean, as it did for pagan thought and for Jewish and Roman law, that the fetus is merely a part of the mother. In another work he appeals to the mother—not to the father, the philosophers or Roman law—to make the pronouncement about a fetus's status:

> In this matter the best teacher, judge, and witness is the sex that is concerned with birth. I call on you, mothers, whether you are now pregnant or have already borne children; let women who are barren and men keep silence! We are looking for the truth about the nature of woman; we are examining the

reality of your pains. Tell us: Do you feel any stirring of life within you in the fetus? Does your groin tremble, your sides shake, your whole stomach throb as the burden you carry changes its position? Are not these moments a source of joy and assurance that the child within you is alive and playful? Should his restlessness subside, would you not be immediately concerned for him?[33]

This last quotation comes from one of Tertullian's later works, *De anima (On the Soul)*. This work, unlike the *Apology*, generally represents the position of Montanism, a strict, enthusiastic movement which he had joined sometime after 200.[34] Although this movement is often considered somewhat heretical, Tertullian's treatment of the soul should be given a fair hearing. Writing in about 210-13, Tertullian attempts to refute all the misunderstandings of the soul which he perceived in pagans and Christians alike. Among these were ideas of the pre-existence of the soul, God's creation of the individual soul at conception, and the infusion of the soul after birth. Tertullian had a notion of the soul as material and argues throughout chapters 23 to 37 that the act of procreation produces both soul and body and that life, therefore, begins at conception. He adduces arguments from medicine, logic and Scripture—including references to Luke 1:41 and 46 and to Jeremiah 1:5:

They [John and Jesus] were both alive while still in the womb. Elizabeth rejoiced as the infant leaped in her womb; Mary glorifies the Lord because Christ within inspired her. Each mother recognizes her child and each is known by her child who is alive, being not merely souls but also spirits.[35]

He continues:

Thus, you read the word of God, spoken to Jeremias: "Before I formed thee in the womb, I knew thee." If God forms us in the womb, He also breathes on us as He did in the beginning: "And God formed man and breathed into him the breath of life." Nor could God have known man in the womb unless he were a whole man. "And before thou camest forth from the womb, I sanctified thee." Was it, then, a dead body at that stage? Surely it was not, for "God is the God of the living and not the dead."[36]

Tertullian is the first Christian to make the explicit connection between these biblical passages and the issue of abortion. Though his main purpose is to prove his particular view of the soul, one of the motives for so doing is to criticize the practice of abortion and to show that even therapeutic abortion is the taking of a human life.[37] For Tertullian, the witness of the Incarnation and of Scripture is to the humanity of the fetus.

A slight change in Tertullian's thought has sometimes been detected near the end of his argument in *De anima*. In chapter 37 he maintains without hesitation that there is

some power, some servant of God's will, which controls the whole process by which the human embryo is implanted in the womb, and there developed and brought to its final form.[38]

He goes on, however, in apparent contradiction of the earlier chapters:

The embryo, therefore, becomes a human being from the moment when its formation is completed. For, Moses imposed punishment in kind for the man who was guilty of causing an abortion on the ground that the embryo was rudimentary "man," exposed to the chances of life and death, since it has already been entered in the book of fate. And this, although it still dwells within the mother and shares with her their mutual life.[39]

On first reading, this reference to the Exodus text on miscarriage seems like a commentary on the formed/unformed distinction present in the Septuagint and an acceptance of the view that the unformed fetus is not human.[40] Since this would contradict the entire argument of the book, however, we need a more satisfactory explanation of this text.

The whole point of chapters 36-37 is that even flesh without specific form can be considered a living being.[41] Although a fetus is not fully formed until just before birth, Moses proves that the fetus is a living "rudimentary 'man' " because he punished in kind (corporally) the one who aborts it. Tertullian, then, refers to Moses' words about form not to distinguish a living from a nonliving fetus but to prove that although the fetus is not *technically* a human being until the whole developmental process is completed, it is to be *considered* a human being because of God's involvement in its development. It is a person-in-process. Tertullian condemns abortion, again appealing to Scripture, and he reiterates the threefold theme of the fetus as a (developing) human under God's care whose abortion is murder and condemnable before God. Furthermore, in a deliberate reference to the opposite position of Roman law, which held that a fetus is never a person, he argues that the fetus is a person in spite of the fact that it is dependent on the mother.[42] Tertullian makes a firm break with Roman law by asserting that the fetus is more than a part of the woman in whom it is found. These views are exactly the same as those expressed in the *Apology*.

Minucius Felix was the only third-century apologist which the West produced. His *Octavius* (ca 200-225), written in Rome during persecutions, is an imaginative attempt to defend Christianity by means of a Ciceronian dialog in which a lawyer mediates between a proponent of Christianity and a proponent of paganism, the latter eventually being converted. After demonstrating the falsehood and immorality of paganism, the Christian addresses himself to the charge that Christian initiations take place by slaughtering a baby. His answer parallels Tertullian's *Apology*, chapter 9. He protests that no one could kill a "tender and so tiny" baby, and that whoever thinks someone could do such a deed must be capable of it himself. Minucius Felix proceeds to accuse the pagans of infanticide and abortion:[43]

And there are women who swallow drugs to stifle in their own womb the beginnings of a man to be—committing infanticide before they give birth to the infant.[44]

The Latin word translated "infanticide" is *parricidium*, the Roman legal word for intentional killing, especially of a relative. Abortion, of course, was not considered parricide in Roman law; Minucius opposes his culture's legal view of abortion. His subsequent assertion that Christians do not procure abortions is necessarily apologetic, but it must have been an accurate generalization of Christian practice to have been of any value to his defense of Christianity.[45]

Abortion in the Church

Although all Christian writers opposed abortion, pagan influence on the church was unavoidable, and abortion was not unknown among "so-called Christians" (the term is Origen's).[46] The situation was recognized as a serious problem by Origen, Hippolytus and Cyprian.

Origen was a teacher, theologian and biblical scholar. Unfortunately, however, his homily on the important text of Exodus 21:22-25 reveals less of Christian teaching and practice than it might. Origen's allegorical method of interpretation makes it difficult to ascertain the specifics of his actual position. Nevertheless, working with the Septuagint, Origen distinguishes between the abortions of unformed and formed fetuses with their corresponding penalties of a fine or a life. That he accepts this fetal distinction as valid is probable but not certain, since he goes on to apply the passage not to abortion but to spiritual harm done to the unformed (catechumens) and formed (baptized persons).[47]

While the apologists praised Christians' refusal to imitate pagan practice, Hippolytus (ca 170-ca 236) was aware of subtle Roman influence on the church and of the church's failure to criticize that influence. Pope Callistus himself approved of a Roman law allowing concubine marriages, even though such marriages often resulted in unwanted pregnancies. Sometime after 222 Hippolytus wrote about the effect of Callistus's laxity:

Women, reputed believers, began to resort to drugs for producing sterility, and to gird themselves round, so to expel

what was being conceived on account of their not wishing to
have a child either by a slave or by any paltry fellow, for the
sake of their family and excessive wealth. Behold, into how
great impiety that lawless one has proceeded, by inculcating
adultery and murder at the same time![48]

In the face of growing immorality, especially among wealthier
believing women, Hippolytus continued to hold forth the orthodox belief that abortion is murder.

Similarly, for Cyprian (ca 200/210-258), orthodox belief and
practice were closely related. This popular writer was not at all
surprised to learn that Novatian was not only schismatic but also
immoral, abusing widows, orphans, his father and even his
wife:

The womb of his wife was smitten by a blow of his heel; and
in the miscarriage that soon followed, the offspring was
brought forth, the fruit of a father's murder. And now he dares
to condemn the hands of those who sacrifice, when he himself
is more guilty in his feet, by which the son, who was about
to be born, was slain?[49]

This text makes the frequent connection between abortion and
guilt.

The theme of guilt and judgment reappears in apocalyptic
texts of the third century. Methodius of Olympus alludes to un-
named "inspired writings," probably the second-century *Apocalypse of Peter*, which promise life to infant victims of abortion
and infanticide, and judgment before Christ to the aborters:

Wherefore have we received it handed down in Scriptures inspired by God *that children who are born before their time, even
if they be the offspring of adultery, are delivered to care-taking
angels.... How could they* have confidently summoned *their
parents* before the judgment seat of Christ *to bring a charge
against them,* saying, *"Thou, O Lord, didst not grudgingly deny
us the light that is common (to all), but these have exposed us to
death, despising thy commandment."*[50]

The text may refer only to infanticide, although "born before their time" was an idiom for abortion. A theology embodying a high view of life is present in this passage: life, according to Methodius, is under God's will and providence from its inception. The passage also sympathizes with the apocalyptic imagery of the children's witness against their guilty parents. Methodius adds the phrase "before the judgment seat of Christ" to the original text, making his position explicitly Christocentric. In the *Apocalypse of Paul*, coming from third-century Egypt (ca 240-250), there is a similar picture of condemnation of those guilty of infanticide (and probably also abortion).[51] These texts reflect the common concern in the early church not only for abortion as infanticide but also for infanticide itself.

Although no texts concerning abortion are available from the second half of the third century, it is safe to assume that the Christian position against abortion continued in a stabilized form throughout that century. The established themes of God's providence for the unborn, abortion as murder and the guilt of those who contribute to abortion remained. At the same time, the question developed of how to deal with believers who had procured abortions. This would be addressed in the next century.

Despite pagan influence on Christians, the late second and early third centuries also give evidence of an increasing Christian effect on Roman law concerning abortion. Although no direct connections between the Christian community and Roman antiabortion laws have been established, several facts suggest at least some influence. First, the Christian position, so different from the Roman view, had spread throughout the empire's geographical regions and social classes. Through the witness of Christians, many pagans were acquainted with their ethical perspective, a perspective similar to that of some pagan moralists, as we saw in chapter two. Second, Christian apologists such as Athenagoras and Tertullian had addressed Roman emperors and governors concerning the standard Christian view. Although before the early third century no Roman legislation appeared which dealt specifically with abortion and abortifacients, at least two significant legal developments occurred in the third century: the enactment of the prescript of Septimus Severus (193-211) and Antoninus Caracalla (211-217), and the application of the *Lex Cornelia* to abortifacient drugs and drug dealers.[52] Is it only coincidental that the apologetic writings of Athenagoras and Tertullian immediately preceded the first Roman laws against abortions? According to the jurist Ulpian, it was the responsibility of governors to exile women who aborted. It has been noted that Septimus Severus legislated against other sex-related crimes and that this may have been due to Christian influence.[53] It seems quite possible that a growing Christian populace influenced public and government opinion toward punishing abortion and promoting life. Perhaps the Romans merely needed ways to counteract the decrease in their population and took advantage of the Christian moral perspective. Whatever the Roman motives may have been, it is difficult to resist the conclusion that Christians contributed to the third-century anti-abortion statutes.

5
CHRISTIANITY ESTABLISHED: THE FOURTH AND FIFTH CENTURIES

AFTER THE "CHRISTIANIZATION" of the Roman Empire under Constantine (313), the practice of abortion undoubtedly increased in the church. According to Epiphanius of Cyprus (ca 315-403), pagan influence was directly responsible for increased use by Christians of contraception and, when that failed, abortion.[1] During the first three centuries, Christian pronouncements about abortion were fundamentally ethical in nature and scope. With the rise of the Christian empire, this strain of thought continued, but legal and speculative theological discussions also took place. During the fourth and early fifth centuries the first ecclesiastical laws against abortion were passed, and five major church Fathers—Basil, Jerome, Ambrose, Augustine and Chrysostom—commented on the practice.

The Councils

The Council of Elvira, in about 305, was the first Christian body to enact punishment for abortion. Nineteen bishops from all over Spain met in this southern Spanish city to decide the fate of the *lapsi*, Christians who had given in to the pressures of persecution, and to seek to prevent the entrance of pagan immorality into the church.[2] Punishments were prescribed for serious sins, ranging from several years of penance to absolute exclusion from Communion even at death.[3] Canons 63 and 68 of that council deal with abortion and infanticide:

> *Canon 63:* If a woman becomes pregnant by committing adultery, while her husband is absent, and after the act she detroys [the child], it is proper to keep her from communion until death, because she has doubled her crime.

> *Canon 68:* If a catechumen should conceive by an adulterer, and should procure the death of the child, she can be baptized only at the end of her life.[4]

Although the original subject of these two canons is not necessarily abortion but perhaps infanticide, canon 63 was applied to abortion by fourth-century writers such as Basil the Great and the compilers of the canons of Ancyra, and it was included with other abortion passages in canon collections of later centuries.[5] The prescribed punishment, penance until death without benefit of Communion even on one's deathbed, applied only to women who aborted and not to husbands or other aides. The reference to an absent husband may mean that the punishment was enacted primarily against wives who aborted to conceal illicit sex. However, since the concern of the canon is not adultery so much as murder, the canon implicitly condemns abortion within premarital or lawful marital relations. Canon 68 prescribes a punishment almost as severe. This severity in penance reflects the general attitude of the early Spanish church and was lightened by later councils.[6]

Did these punishments equate abortion with murder? It is difficult to say, since the penalties enacted by Elvira were based on various moral and social biases. Canon 5 prescribes seven years of penance for purposely striking a servant who subsequently dies, and five years of penance for accidentally doing it. Five years of penance are also prescribed for single acts of adultery (canons 47 and 78) and for continuous unfaithfulness (canon 69). Sodomites are never to be allowed Communion again (canon 71). Thus abortion seems to have been considered more serious than the death of a slave and as serious as sexual perversion. It is probable that this local synod viewed abortion as a combination of adultery and murder, punishable by the gravest penalty. Despite this severity, Elvira and most Christians did not exact the death penalty for any sin, including abortion, although the theologian Ephraem the Syrian (ca 306-373) recommended capital punishment for abortion.[7]

In 314, another council of bishops met at Ancyra, capital of Galatia in Asia Minor. This council was geographically wider in scope than Elvira, including the churches of both Asia Minor and Syria. The council's purpose was again to deal with the *lapsi* of recent persecutions, those who had participated in pagan idolatry and immorality. The council wrote concerning infanticide and abortion:

Canon 21: Women who prostitute themselves, and who kill the children thus begotten, or who try to destroy them when in their wombs, are by ancient law excommunicated to the end of their lives. We, however, have softened their punishment, and condemned them to the various appointed degrees of penance for ten years.[8]

This text changes an earlier legal punishment, probably that of Elvira, from life excommunication to one of ten years' time.[9] However, the immorality of abortion is not questioned nor its seriousness diminished. Once Christianity introduced a legal system, it, like Judaism, sometimes maintained a distinction between moral and legal evaluations. Legally, abortion was classified somewhere between unpremeditated murder and adultery, each punishable for five to seven years (canons 20 and

23), and willful murder, punishable for life (canon 22). One textual variant indicates that some people preferred the earlier lifelong punishment; another suggests that the same ten-year punishment may have been inflicted on accomplices.

The Council of Ancyra was important because of its ten-year penalty, which continued as standard into the Middle Ages. The introduction of the verb *try* into the text may well have been an effort to punish attempted as well as successful abortions; this was the common interpretation in subsequent centuries.[10] Ancyra was important for later theology: first, because it made no distinction between the formed and unformed fetus; second, because it said nothing about those who helped or forced women to abort. These two aspects of Ancyra paved the way for one of the most profound theological and ethical statements on abortion during the first four centuries, made in a letter from Basil the Great to Amphilochius, bishop of Iconium.

The Fathers

Basil of Caesarea (ca 330-379), one of the Cappadocian Fathers, was a superb administrator, an orthodox theologian, a liturgical reformer and the founder of Eastern monasticism. His writings were read and appreciated by pagans and Christians alike.[11] His dogmatic and devotional activities centered on the purity and unity of the church, and his numerous letters give important information on the church in his day.

In 374 Basil wrote to Amphilochius to answer questions raised by the bishop about church order and moral problems. One question concerned murder. In his response, Basil included the following statement on abortion:

She who has deliberately destroyed a fetus has to pay the penalty of murder. And there is no exact inquiry among us as to whether the fetus was formed or unformed. For, here it is not only the child to be born that is vindicated, but also the woman herself who made an attempt against her own life, because usually the women die in such attempts. Furthermore, added to this is the destruction of the embryo, another murder, at least according to the intention of those who dare these things. Nevertheless, we should not prolong their penance until death, but should accept a term of ten years, and we should determine the treatment not by time, but by the manner of repentance.[12]

Here Basil removes any notion of legalism which would minimize either the seriousness of abortion or the grace of God. First, he dismisses as irrelevant all casuistic distinctions between the formed and the unformed fetus. For him, intention matters above all because all life—that of the fetus and that of the mother —is sacred. Second, he recognizes the value and necessity of condemning abortion as a crime as well as a sin, but he views sincere repentance as a valid sign of God's grace and forgiveness.[13] Abortion is not to be seen as the unforgivable sin, but it has to be considered a serious disregard for human life which usually results in two murders.[14]

Later in the same letter Basil condemns those who help women to abort:

Moreover, those, too, who give drugs causing abortion are [deliberate murderers] themselves, as well as those receiving the poison which kills the fetus.[15]

Basil the Great, then, condemns all abortion as murder, a sin to be judged by God through the church but also to be forgiven by his grace.

A great Western Father indebted to Basil was Ambrose (ca 339-397). This well-educated rhetorician and bishop of Milan modeled his preaching during Holy Week of 387 on a series of Basil's sermons on creation. In a sermon on the fifth day of creation about the wonders of birds and their example to humanity, Ambrose criticizes "females of our species" for not nursing their own children (the rich) and for exposing them (the poor). The wealthy, especially, are also guilty of abortion:

The wealthy, in order that their inheritance may not be divided among several, deny in the very womb their own progeny. By use of parricidal mixtures they snuff out the fruit of their wombs in the genital organs themselves. In this way life is taken away before it is given. . . . Who except man himself has taught us ways of repudiating children?[16]

In another context, discussing the procreative purpose of sex, Ambrose exalts the unborn child as God's handiwork:

It is written: "Before I formed you in the womb I knew you, and in the genitals of your mother I sanctified you" (Jer 1:5). To inhibit your rashness, you are made to notice that the hands of your maker are forming something in the womb into a man.[17]

Ambrose focuses on the common Christian understanding of the care and providence of God in forming the fetus in the womb and the utter disrespect for God expressed by abortion.

A Western contemporary of Basil was the learned doctor of the church Jerome (ca 342-420), known for his scholarly abilities as well as for being an "uncompromising and outspoken critic of contemporary morals."[18] In one of his most famous letters, written in 384, Jerome makes graphic observations on Roman society and its effect on "Mother Church," who daily loses unmarried women to immorality, for they

drink potions to ensure sterility and are guilty of murdering a human being not yet conceived. Some, when they learn they are with child through sin, practice abortion by the use of drugs. Frequently they die themselves and are brought before the rulers of the lower world guilty of three crimes: suicide, adultery against Christ, and murder of an unborn child.[19]

Origen had raised a similar concern over sterilizing drugs as an expression of his theology of marriage; here Jerome demonstrates concern over their relationship to illicit sex. A more important issue to Jerome, however, is abortion, especially when practiced by women who have conceived outside of marriage. This he forcefully condemns in his letter. The traditional themes of murder and guilt reappear. Jerome introduces a new perspective by explicitly calling a woman's own abortion-induced death "suicide." His other contribution is to take from the Bible the relationship between physical and spiritual adultery and to associate it with abortion by an unmarried woman.

Like Tertullian before and Augustine after, Jerome distinguished between the formed and the unformed fetus and said that a certain stage of development is necessary before there is a person and, hence, before there can be a murder.[20] This distinction received much more attention and approval in the West than in the East.

Contemporary with Basil, Ambrose and Jerome was a manual of Christian life and behavior compiled in Syria (ca 380). It was indebted in form and content to two second-century works, the *Epistle of Barnabas* and the *Didache*, and came to be called the *Apostolic Constitutions* or the *Constitutions of the Holy Apostles*.[21] In a list of immoral practices including illicit sexual relations, magic, witchcraft and fraud, this statement appears:

> Thou shalt not slay thy child by causing abortion, nor kill that which is begotten. For every thing that is shaped, and hath received a soul from God, if it be slain, shall be avenged, as being unjustly destroyed.[22]

This text, though parallel to the Way of Life in the *Didache* in its condemnation of abortion and infanticide, makes an addition— the idea of a fetal soul—that was unknown to early second-century Christianity and rare in fourth-century Eastern Christianity. The second sentence of the text may distinguish between the formed and the unformed fetus, although it may merely comment on the nature of both the born and the unborn child as shaped and given a soul by God. Even if the distinction is made, the themes of murder and the providential work of God remain. And, as in the *Didache* and the *Epistle of Barnabas*, the Way of Death includes "murderers of infants" and "destroyers of the workmanship of God."[23]

Thus the Christian position first articulated in the early second century survived through the fourth. Despite an increasing problem within its borders, which now included much of the populace, the church managed to maintain its ethical position, giving only occasional leeway on the question of abortion as murder to those who distinguished between the formed and the unformed fetus. The late fourth and early fifth centuries produced two great commentators on the subject, one expressing the "liberal" and one the "strict" view.

Augustine and Chrysostom

Both Augustine (354-430) and Chrysostom (ca 347-407), the early church's greatest theologian in the West and greatest preacher in the East, condemned abortion. However, their approaches to the issue and their specific answers reflected in almost stereotypical fashion the differences between theologians and preachers and between West and East.

No church Father gave more attention to the topic of abortion than did Augustine, and no church Father has received more attention concerning his position on abortion than he has. Augustine's view must not be removed from the context of his struggles to understand the origin of life, original sin and marriage. Augustine fluctuated on the question of the soul's origin. He seems to have thought at various times that it is pre-existent, that it comes from the parents like the body, that it is created and given by God at conception, or that it is infused at the point of formation.[24] Generally, he did distinguish between the unformed and the formed, animate human embryo. Augustine also believed that original sin was transmitted from parents to child through the lustful aspects of sexual intercourse; without baptism, a child was damned. Nevertheless, he believed in the goodness of marriage and sex as long as their "end and aim"—childbearing—was promoted.[25]

For Augustine the destruction of a formed fetus was murder, but the destruction of an unformed fetus, though immoral and worthy of a fine, was not murder.[26] Furthermore, he opposed contraceptive and sterilizing drugs as well as abortifacients on the grounds that all three deny the purpose of sex and marriage:

Sometimes, indeed, this lustful cruelty, or if you please, cruel lust, resorts to such extravagant methods as to use poisonous drugs to secure barrenness; or else, if unsuccessful in this, to destroy the conceived seed by some means previous to birth, preferring that its offspring should rather perish than receive vitality; or if it was advancing to life within the womb, should be slain before it was born.[27]

Augustine here condemns sterilization and distinguishes between abortion of the unformed and abortion of the formed fetus.

Despite his connection between sterilization or contraception and abortion, Augustine's position on abortion was not based solely on his theology of marriage (which modern readers might easily refute). He held a high view of life as the work of God from its inception. This more profound reason for his condemnation of abortion seems to have made him uncomfortable with his distinctions between the formed and the unformed fetus. In the *Enchiridion* (421), his famed handbook on the Catholic faith, he discusses the fate of aborted fetuses in light of his convictions about the resurrection to eternal life. He admits that it is natural to think that an undeveloped fetus would perish "like seeds that did not germinate."[28] Immediately, however, he checks this assumption:

But who, then, would dare to deny—though he would not dare to affirm it either—that in the resurrection day what is lacking in the forms of things will be filled out? Thus, the perfection which time would have accomplished will not be lacking. . . . Nature, then, will be cheated of nothing apt and fitting which time's passage would have brought. . . . What is not yet whole will become whole.[29]

Augustine thus reconsiders the logical consequences of his doctrines of the soul and of original sin. When does a fetus become human? If it is aborted, will it be damned? He also examines the extremely difficult question of therapeutic abortion:

To deny, for example, that those fetuses ever lived at all which

are cut away limb by limb and cast out of the wombs of pregnant women, lest the mothers die also if the fetuses were left
there dead, would seem much too rash.[30]

Augustine's method of handling abortion from a theological
perspective changed as his thought matured and found expression in the *Enchiridion*. Speculation about the origin of the soul,
about the human and nonhuman fetus, about the meaning of
original sin now gave way to his long-held conviction that all
human life is "God's own work."[31] Faced with human inability
to ascertain when the fetus begins to live, Augustine chose to
emphasize the value of all life, whether actual or potential.

John Chrysostom, on the other hand, was an example of impassioned moral conviction. His sermons in the late fourth and
very early fifth centuries, which later earned him the name
Chrysostom ("golden-mouthed"), thundered against moral laxity
in society and the church. In a forceful sermon on Romans 13:
11-14, while denouncing the evils of drunkenness and fornication, Chrysostom vividly condemns abortion:

Why sow where the ground makes it its care to destroy the
fruit? where there are many efforts at abortion? where there
is murder before the birth? for even the harlot thou dost not
let continue a mere harlot, but makest her a murderer also.
You see how drunkenness leads to whoredom, whoredom to
adultery, adultery to murder; or rather to something even
worse than murder. For I have no name to give it, since it does
not take off the thing born, but prevents its being born. Why
then dost thou abuse the gift of God, and fight with His laws,
and follow after what is a curse as if a blessing, and make the
chamber of procreation a chamber for murder, and arm the
woman that was given for childbearing unto slaughter? For
with a view to drawing more money by being agreeable and
an object of longing to her lovers, even this she is not back-
ward to do, so heaping upon thy head a great pile of fire. For
even if the daring deed be hers, yet the causing of it is thine.
Hence too come idolatries, since many, with a view to become

acceptable, devise incantations, and libations, and love-potions, and countless other plans. Yet still after such great unseemliness, after slaughters, after idolatries, the thing [fornication] seems to many to belong to things indifferent, aye, and to many that have wives, too.[32]

Chrysostom combines the themes of his predecessors: he associates abortion with sexual immorality, calls it murder, makes known the punishment it deserves and sees the fetus as an object of God's care. In fact, Chrysostom's profound abhorrence of abortion leads him to classify it as "something even worse than murder."

Is there a solution to this spiritual and moral evil? Chrysostom, quoting Romans 13:14, answers:

Let us put on Christ, and be with Him continually... having Him evermore visible in us.[33]

Augustine the theologian and Chrysostom the preacher approached abortion from very different perspectives. For Augustine, it was a case of moral and theological ambiguity. For Chrysostom, it was a clear-cut moral evil. Yet both, like Basil, saw the marvelous grace of God in creation and redemption, a vision which compelled each of them to affirm God's care for human life even before birth.

We have seen that despite legal and theological disputes, Christians of the fourth and early fifth centuries maintained the earliest Christian stance against abortion. In addition, they introduced the theme of forgiveness and grace for those who had obtained abortions. In the next chapter we will examine various forces which contributed to the basic Christian position.

6
ABORTION AND THE EARLY CHURCH: THE WIDER CONTEXT

THE EARLY CHRISTIANS WERE NOT alone in opposing abortion; pagans and Jews also opposed it for various reasons. The Christian position was developed in the context of Greco-Roman culture as well as in the context of other aspects of Christian faith and life. To understand the motives for the early Christian position on abortion, we must compare Christian and non-Christian reasons for opposing it. We must also consider the relationship of the Christian antiabortion stand to other Christian ethical beliefs.

The Cultural Context
A careful inquiry into ancient sources reveals that the Christian condemnation of abortion shared some elements with condemnations by pagans and Jews. Nevertheless, distinctive features in the Christian view did emerge.

Concern about abortion was shared by Christians with outspoken pagans in the fields of medicine, law, rhetoric, philosophy and religion. Pagans and Christians alike criticized the use of abortion to conceal sexual immorality or as a means of birth control. Both groups cared about the safety of the woman who took poisons or used mechanical means to attempt to abort. Again, both pagans and Christians occasionally appealed to the animal kingdom for examples of the natural parental instinct which those who practiced abortion or exposure willfully ignored.

These basic parallels have given rise to the suggestion that the Christian position was a direct borrowing from pagan sources. The Platonic belief that the fetus is a living being endowed with a soul is held to be one such possible source.[1] While this belief may have aided some Christians in expressing their antiabortion convictions, the belief itself fails to explain fully the Christian opposition; Plato himself supported abortion in certain situations. Moreover, Platonic discussion about the fetus was more speculative than ethical. If Platonic ideas influenced Christian thought, Christians supplemented those ideas to form their own distinct position.

Another possible source of Christian opposition to abortion is the apocalyptic imagery of damnation found in certain pagan religious traditions from the East and from Egypt, traditions which also believed that the fetus has a soul.[2] Some hold that early Christian fear of the loss of an unbaptized soul, even the soul of a fetus, came from these sources, resulting in Christian protest against abortion and infanticide.[3] But only two Christian documents (the *Apocalypse of Peter* and the *Apocalypse of Paul*), make any attempt to link abortion with hellfire and brimstone. Furthermore, the Christian apocalypses, unlike their prototypes, portray the unborn not as the judged but as those who judge their murderers. Inasmuch as Christians displayed no fear that an aborted fetus would be condemned, pagan apocalyptic imagery could not have been the source of Christian opposition to abortion. Christians rather borrowed such imagery and transformed it into one manifestation of that opposition.

It has also been suggested that the early Christians adopted the ethical thinking of certain pagan moralists, particularly the Stoics.[4] Indeed, the Stoics disapproved of abortion, but their reasons must be considered. Musonius Rufus, a typical example, rejected abortion as part of his larger theory that procreation is the natural and sole purpose of sex. Abortion went contrary to his support of the rightness, beauty and profit of large families. For him, abortion was an attack against sex, marriage, the father and even the gods, but not against the fetus. This lack of specific concern for the unborn sets the Stoic position apart from the Christian view.[5]

Concern for the fetus distinguishes the Christian position from all pagan disapproval of abortion. Pagan antiabortion statements are consistently mindful of the welfare and rights of the state, the father, the family and even occasionally the woman, but never those of the fetus. Even religious prohibitions are motivated only by concern for the woman's ritual purity.[6] When compared to pagan opinion, the most distinctive feature of early Christian rejection of abortion is its placing the well-being of the fetus at the center of the issue. Christians discarded all pagan definitions of the fetus as merely part of the mother's body. To Christians, the fetus was an independent living being. They consequently repudiated any utilitarian notion of the nature of the fetus; in the abortion discussion, they always considered the unborn as God's creation.

Moreover, notable differences prevailed in the very structure of pagan and Christian ethical systems. The pagan ethic most important to early Christianity was Stoicism. Similarities between the two were numerous, and Christians were indebted in many ways to the Stoics. There was, however, one crucial difference. Stoic ethical views were expressed in the form of diatribes, well-organized rhetorical essays in which questions were answered and arguments made about right and natural acts, but no behavior was demanded. Christian ethics, on the other hand, was fundamentally imperatival, consisting of commands understood to be the Word of the living Lord. This did not mean that Christianity provided no freedom for personal decision, but rather that all of life, including ethical decisions, was understood to be a response to God. The early Christian discussion of abortion is rooted firmly in the conviction that abortion is a matter of "thou shalt" and "thou shalt not." Even in those statements which are not in a specific commandment form, the imperative is implicitly present.

Before we leave the subject of Stoic influence on Christians to investigate Jewish influence, we must consider two issues whose importance was understood by both Stoics and Jews: the purpose of marriage and the morality of contraception.

The Stoics believed that marriage had two purposes, community *(koinōnia)* between husband and wife, and procreation.[7] Similarly the Jews saw marriage as companionship which was obligated to procreate.[8] For both Stoics and Jews, procreation seems to have been the more important of the two purposes. The Stoics, however, held that sexual intercourse had only one natural purpose, procreation; it was not to be engaged in for pleasure.[9] The Jews, while stressing the duty to have children, believed that sex was both a duty and a legitimate pleasure in and of itself.[10]

The Stoics, therefore, in their rejection of sex for nonprocreative reasons, implicitly rejected contraception. The Jews, on the other hand, did not spurn contraception because of any opposition to marital sex for pleasure, but they did disapprove of those forms (and only those forms) of contraception which prevented the flow of the seed into the woman's body. Such means of contraception were believed to corrupt or destroy the seed and hence life itself.[11]

The earliest Christians, as seen through the New Testament, apparently did not copy either Stoic or Jewish views on sex. Unlike the Stoics, Christians did not consider procreation the sole purpose of sex in marriage.[12] Christians agreed with Jewish ideas about the goodness and obligations of marital sex, but they also placed high value on the alternative of celibacy as a means of serving the kingdom of God.[13] As time passed, however, a shift occurred. By the end of the second century, Christians had generally accepted a combination of Stoic and Jewish beliefs coupled with some unique Christian features. The chief purpose of marriage and the sole purpose of sex, they believed, was procreation. They did not accept the idea of sex for pleasure alone, and they condemned contraception. They became convinced that the best way of life for Christians was celibacy.[14]

Several significant reasons for this shift must be noted. First, Christians were disturbed by the fact that many contraceptives were classified as magic or poison, dispensed by practitioners of sorcery.[15] Second, the new view was a reaction to the lust and moral laxity of the age; like abortion, contraception was used to cover rampant immorality. Third, Christians were repulsed by the sexually libertine lifestyles of some Gnostics.[16] Certain Gnostic groups even indulged in nonprocreative intercourse, using various contraceptive techniques, during religious ceremonies.[17]

Most important of all, Christians of the late second century and subsequent eras had to answer the extreme ascetic tendencies of many of the flourishing Gnostic groups and later the abhorrence of procreation by the dualistic Manichees. For these groups, both marriage and sex were forms of immorality, things to be escaped, not sought. The Gnostics pressed various New Testament passages to defend their rejection of marriage, while the Manichees blamed procreation for the evil and darkness in the world.[18] Orthodox Christians were forced to respond; some emphasized the Christian ideal of marriage as a mirror of Christ and the church, but most, beginning with the Apologists, tried to restore sex and marriage to a place of respect by claiming that their purpose is procreation alone.[19] Logically, they condemned contraception as an assault on the sanctity and purpose of sex and marriage.

The question now arises: Did Christians outlaw abortion merely because it was a frustration of the purpose of sex and a means of contraception? What was the relationship between abortion and contraception in the eyes of the early Christians? Christians sometimes prohibited abortion and contraception in the same context. This was the case in the earliest Christian writings against drugs and magic, as well as in writings which condemned both abortion and contraception as means of concealing immorality. In addition, taking sterilizing drugs and having sexual intercourse during pregnancy were sometimes seen, like abortion, as means of preventing or attacking human life. Condemnation of abortion and contraception originally appeared, however, at different times, for different reasons and in different contexts.

In the first place, writings against abortion predate both the first statements about contraception and the appearance of the "procreation only" theme. Explicit condemnation of abortion dates from no later than the early second century (*Didache, Epistle of Barnabas, Apocalypse of Peter*), whereas the first explicit reference to contraception does not occur before the third century in the writings of Hippolytus.[20] Even this reference to "drugs for producing sterility," however, may be a poor translation of a technical term for abortive drugs.[21] In fact, many of the supposed early Christian references to contraception are more likely references either to abortifacients or to acts such as castration, homosexual intercourse or masturbation which are contraceptive only incidentally.[22] More frequent than specific references to contraception are references to the procreative purpose of sex and to the avoidance by some people of its proper use.[23] Such statements, which implicitly ban contraception, begin to appear about fifty years after the first writings on abortion. This lack of material on contraception contrasts with the abundance of material on abortion.

That Christians separated their views on contraception from their views on abortion is further evidenced by their reasons for addressing each topic. Rejection of contraception and emphasis on procreation spoke to perceived abuses within the broad Christian community in an attempt to strengthen that community's belief in the sanctity of sex and of marriage. Disapproval of abortion, on the other hand, arose in reaction to practices of the surrounding culture, not those of the church; it expresssed a new concern for the sanctity of unborn life. Though a tacit connection between the two may have existed, concern for procreation necessarily yielding concern for the unborn, and vice versa, Christians did not see the destruction of the fetus merely as the frustration of the natural result of sexual intercourse.[24]

Finally, abortion and contraception are generally discussed in different immediate contexts. Abortion is almost always mentioned along with some form of violence; in fact, it is considered a subdivision of the general categories of violence, murder and infanticide. Contraception, however, is usually discussed along with the procreative purpose of marriage and the call to deny pleasure.

Early Christian opposition to abortion, then, did not arise because abortion was seen as a means of interrupting the natural course of sexual relations but because it was viewed as murder. Denunciation of abortion developed prior to and independently of opposition to contraception. Opposition to contraception was not derived from antiabortionism, which reacted to a common practice in the surrounding culture, but arose rather in response to problems in the Christian community.[25] One reason early Christians reacted strongly to the abuse of contraception and sex was the high value they placed on marriage, sex, conception and birth, which they respected as sacred aspects of life.

Whereas Stoic ideas had the greatest influence on the church's developing positions on sex and contraception, Jewish ideas dominated their position on abortion. The sanctity of life was a

fundamental tenet of Judaism. Jews considered the fetus a creation of God, not to be purposely harmed. Justice toward the
helpless and innocent stood at the center of Jewish ethics. Above
all, the Jewish horror of bloodshed impressed itself upon the
early Christians, molding their various ethical perspectives into
one unified position.

In the early centuries of Christianity, an important distinction
developed between Jewish and Christian ethics. Christianity
did not at first establish a religious and legal political society
with laws; consequently, Christians did not distinguish legal
from ethical perspectives on the fetus. Without concern for ritual
impurity and legal definitions, they developed a more forceful
and blanket condemnation of abortion than did the Jews, not
hesitating to call it murder. The Christian view of abortion thus
arose out of a Jewish ethical environment but transcended and
transformed that ethic.

In short, Christians were not alone in opposing abortion; they
were accompanied and influenced by both pagans and Jews. An
examination of non-Christian sources and influences, however,
does not fully explain why the early Christians opposed abortion. What was present in the new faith itself that caused the
early Christians to agree with aspects of pagan and especially
Jewish ethics? What prompted them both to maintain and to
transform the ethics which influenced them most? Answers to
these questions must be sought in the early Christian writings
themselves.

The Ethical Context
The early Christian love for life and abhorrence of bloodshed,
both inherited from the Jews, contrasted sharply with the violence and disrespect for human life which stained the pagan
culture around them. The helpless of pagan society (slaves, the
poor, women and children) were often disdained or maltreated.
The Greco-Roman world demonstrated its depreciation of life in
its wars, gladiator fights, innumerable crucifixions, exposure of

the newborn and abortion of the unborn. Christians interpreted their society's attitude as a choice in favor of bloodshed over love. If society preferred the way of bloodshed, Christians chose the way of love expressed concretely through nonviolence and compassionate justice.

Jesus' own life and teachings were the basis of this lifestyle. He had not only commanded his followers, "Love your neighbor as yourself"; he had also redefined the concept of neighbor to include even one's enemy:

You have heard that it was said, "You shall love your neighbor and hate your enemy." But I say to you, Love your enemies and pray for those who persecute you, so that you may be sons of your Father who is in heaven; for he makes his sun rise on the evil and on the good, and sends rain on the just and on the unjust. For if you love those who love you, what reward have you? Do not even the tax collectors do the same? And if you salute only your brethren, what more are you doing than others? Do not even the Gentiles do the same? You, therefore, must be perfect, as your heavenly Father is perfect. (Mt 5:43-48)

Throughout his life and even during the horror of his trial, crucifixion and death, Jesus consistently exhibited this type of neighbor love toward all he encountered. He permitted no violence in bringing about the kingdom of God but insisted that "all who take the sword will perish by the sword" (Mt 26:52b). He called his disciples to be peacemakers (Mt 5:9).

Jesus also enjoined his followers to love and provide for the weak, the poor and the oppressed. This theme was not new; he simply continued the Old Testament's representation of God's inherent justice that should also characterize his people. Jesus was known for his unusual love for society's outcasts: lepers, the poor, women, children and others whom the Romans and even some Jews despised and neglected.

Jesus' example and command stirred early Christians; they followed his example seriously and literally. As Tertullian and Irenaeus explained, their obedience to his love commands resulted in practical demonstrations of concern

> for feeding and burying the poor, for boys and girls destitute of property and parents; and further for old people confined to the house, and victims of shipwreck; and any who are in the mines, who are exiled to an island, or who are in prison merely on account of God's church.[26]

> And instead of the tithes which the law commanded, the Lord said to divide everything we have with the poor. And he said to love not only our neighbors but also our enemies, and to be givers and sharers not only with the good but also to be liberal givers toward those who take away our possessions.[27]

Christians demonstrated love not only to fellow Christians but also to those outside the community and even to those who opposed the faith. This lifestyle of love became intimately connected with the issue of nonviolence. The link between the two is clearly expressed by Clement of Alexandria in an address to wealthy Christians. He exhorts the rich to abandon the Roman custom of buying one's own legions and to form instead a nonwarring "army" of the poor and weak by providing for their needs:

> Contrary to the rest of men enlist for yourself an army without weapons, without war, without bloodshed, without wrath, without stain—pious old men, orphans dear to God, widows armed with gentleness, men adorned with love. Obtain with your wealth as guards of body and soul such as these whose commander is God.[28]

Clement's statement is not extraordinary; it concisely represents the entire body of Christian literature from the first three centuries by affirming that Christian discipleship and love demand a complete renunciation of violence and bloodshed. Jesus' new definition of *neighbor* yielded an ethical stance unique to the ancient world. All distinctions between people—Gentile and Jew, man and woman, adult and child, slave and free, rich and poor, guilty and innocent—were obliterated by the commands to love all and to forsake violence. All people are one's neighbors; therefore the blood of none may be shed. Bloodshed of any kind was equated with murder, which, along with idolatry and immorality, became known as one of the three mortal sins. Those guilty of bloodshed were to be excommunicated from the Christian community.[29]

The practical consequence of this revolutionary attitude was that Christians refused to watch or participate in revenge, violence or bloodshed of any kind, whether in a personal or social context, as Origen explained:

If a revolt had been the cause of the Christians existing as a separate group (and they originated from the Jews for whom it was lawful to take up arms in defense of their families and to serve in wars), the lawgiver of the Christians [Jesus] would not have forbidden entirely the taking of human life. He taught that it was never right for his disciples to go so far against a man, even if he should be very wicked; for he did not consider it compatible with his inspired legislation to allow the taking of human life in any form at all. Moreover, if Christians had originated from a revolt, they would not have submitted to laws which were so gentle, which caused them to be killed "as sheep," and made them unable ever to defend themselves against their persecutors.[30]

Tertullian wrote that according to Christian doctrine, "greater permission is given to be killed than to kill."[31]

Christians extended this prohibition of bloodshed specifically to acts such as infant exposure, infanticide and gladiator fights. They also forbade capital punishment. Lactantius wrote:

When God forbids us to kill, he not only prohibits us from open violence, which is not even allowed by the public laws, but he warns us against the commission of those things which are esteemed lawful among men. Thus it will be neither lawful for a just man to engage in warfare, since his warfare is justice itself, nor to accuse anyone of a capital charge, because it makes no difference, whether you put a man to death by word, or rather by sword, since it is the act of putting to death itself which is prohibited. Therefore, with regard to this precept of God, there ought to be no exception at all, but that it is always unlawful to put to death a man, whom God willed to be a sacred animal.[32]

Watching an execution was considered no less defiling than participating in one.[33]

Logically consistent with this view was the early Christian opposition to military service and war. Several important modern works discuss the issue of war and peace in the early church and demonstrate that pacifism was indeed the official and accepted position of Christians until the time of Constantine.[34] Conversion to Christ meant conversion from war to peace:

[We] were filled full of war, and slaughter one of another, and every kind of evil, [and] have from out of the whole earth each changed our weapons of war, our swords into ploughshares and our pikes into farming tools, and we farm piety, righteousness, the love of man, faith, and hope which comes from the Father himself through him who was crucified.[35]

The early Christians believed that through and in Christ and his people the Old Testament prophecies of eschatological peace had been fulfilled. Those who followed the Prince of Peace could no longer engage in war. Tertullian argued this forcefully:

Shall it be held lawful to make an occupation of the sword when the Lord proclaims that he who makes use of the sword shall perish by the sword? And shall the son of peace take part in the battle when it is not proper for him even to go to law?[36]

But now inquiry is made about this point, whether a believer is able to turn himself to military service and whether the soldier may be admitted unto the faith, even the ordinary soldier or the lower ranks, to whom there is no necessity for taking part in sacrifices or capital punishments? There is no agreement between the divine and the human oath, the standard of Christ and the standard of the devil, the camp of light

and the camp of darkness. One soul cannot be under obliga-
tion to two, God and Caesar. . . . But how will a Christian war,
indeed how will he serve even in peace without a sword,
which the Lord has taken away? . . . The Lord, in disarming
Peter, unbelted every soldier.[37]

In acknowledging the one God as Creator of the whole world
and Jesus as their only King, Christians could no longer pledge
complete allegiance to their own nation, for they realized that
they were part of a common humanity and a common universal
fellowship of Christians:

For what are the interests of our country, but the inconveni-
ences of another state or nation?—that is, to extend the
boundaries which are evidently taken from others, to increase
the power of the state, to improve the revenues—all which
things are not virtues, but the overthrowing of virtues; for in
the first place, the union of human society is taken away, the
abstaining from the property of another is taken away; lastly,
justice itself is taken away, which is unable to bear the tearing
asunder of the human race, and wherever arms have glittered,
must be banished and exterminated from thence. For how can
a man be just who injures, who hates, who despoils, who
puts to death? and they who strive to be serviceable to their
country do all these things.[38]

Is the laurel of triumph made up of leaves, or of corpses?
is it decorated with ribbons, or tombs? is it besmeared with
ointments, or with the tears of wives and mothers, perhaps
those of some men even (who are) Christians—for Christ (is)
among the barbarians as well?[39]

Many partial explanations for Christian nonparticipation in the
army have been suggested, such as the army's unconditional
oath to and worship of Caesar, its worship of pagan gods, the
brutality and general behavior of soldiers and their duty to exe-
cute the death penalty.[40] Yet, as Roland Bainton infers from
Tertullian, Christian soldiers could have avoided the oaths,
Caesar-worship and even actual killing in peacetime.[41] Some

early theologians therefore condemned only participation in war itself and not military service per se.[42]

At the root of the Christian refusal to join the army, however, was the army's connection with bloodshed. The army's very essence was defiled by killing; most Christians therefore could not consider army service a justifiable occupation. Special provisions for soldiers who became Christians had to be made; if they could avoid idolatry and bloodshed, they could remain soldiers. Those who were already or wished to become Christians, on the other hand, were usually urged not to join the army and were sometimes threatened with excommunication if they did.[43]

Although this Christ-centered pacifism was the standard of the early church, some Christians did in fact join the military, and some did fight.[44] Nevertheless, the widespread attestation of early Christian pacifism discloses the church's original adherence to the nonviolent love ethic lived and taught by Jesus. Christian nonparticipation in the army or in warfare did not mean nonparticipation in society. Rather, Christians desired to function in society as bearers of truth, love, justice and peace rather than bearers of bloodshed. Although some early Christian writers even promised to pray for their nation's just causes, they would not participate in killing a fellow human being.[45]

As time went on, the church began to slip from its early pacifism. More Christians became soldiers in the third than in the second century.[46] The marriage of church and state under Constantine allowed for the development of the just war theory. This theory, intimating that Christians could and should participate in certain wars, was expressed most clearly by Augustine.[47] By 416, not only were Christians joining the army en masse, but the emperor Theodosius II, in order to secure the blessing of God on his battles, declared that *only* Christians could be in the army.[48] A remnant of pacifists remained in the church after Constantine, but the general consensus moved to favor Christian participation in just wars.[49] What had once been labeled violent and murderous became right, good and even obligatory.

The same writers who opposed bloodshed in any other form also condemned abortion: the authors of the *Didache* and the *Epistle of Barnabas*, Athenagoras, Clement of Alexandria, Tertullian, Origen, Hippolytus, Minucius Felix and Cyprian. For these people the love which obliterated distinctions between adult and child, guilty and innocent, friend and enemy also demolished the distinction between born and unborn. Christ's life and teachings raised the fetus to the status of neighbor. Abortion manifested violence and injustice to that neighbor and thus became an example of bloodshed, or murder. Those who refused to kill in war refused to kill in the womb, and vice versa.

The Christian case against abortion proceeded, it seems, in this manner: Jesus taught and lived a life of love for the neighbor, especially the weak, the innocent, children and women. He also exemplified a life of nonviolence, refusing to take life, teaching that God is the Creator of all and that any form of attack on another is murder. The unborn child is a human life, a neighbor. Violence against the fetus, therefore, is violence against one's neighbor, and the shedding of the blood of the fetus is murder of one's neighbor, the ultimate lack of love.

Since Christians saw abortion in the wider context of bloodshed, murder and lack of neighbor love, they of course argued against it as well as these. The *Didache* and *Epistle of Barnabas* contrast abortion with neighbor love, branding abortion as an example of murder and social injustice. Athenagoras claims that consistent Christian belief dismisses *all* forms of violence. Tertullian introduces his discussion of abortion with the words "in our case, murder being once for all forbidden."[50]

In this earliest period, Christians were unable to separate abortion from violence in general.[51] As their antiabortion position became established, they no longer always needed to compare abortion with other forms of bloodshed in order to make their point. After the time of Constantine, however, abortion continued to be condemned though warfare was condoned.[52]

The doctrine of the just war finally severed the original connection between abortion and participation in war as two unacceptable forms of bloodshed.

The earliest Christian ethic, from Jesus to Constantine, can be described as a consistent pro-life ethic. It was in favor of human life regardless of age, nationality or social standing. It pleaded for the poor, the weak, women, children and the unborn. This pro-life ethic discarded hate in favor of love, war in favor of peace, oppression in favor of justice, bloodshed in favor of life. The Christian's response to abortion was one important aspect of this consistent pro-life ethic. Rooted in Jewish love for life and hatred of bloodshed, it developed a specific Christian character as part of early Christian holistic discipleship. To follow Jesus was to forsake bloodshed.

7
THE RELEVANCE OF THE EARLY CHURCH FOR TODAY

FOR CHRISTIANS, THE DOCTRINE OF THE church universal demands careful attention to Christians of other times as well as other places. As one modern theologian has said, "Theology is a conversation with living voices of the past and present."[1] The special importance of early church history is undeniable. This was the period when a fresh new faith captured people's minds and hearts. Living the new faith in a pagan environment proved challenging and stimulating as the many implications of Christianity unfolded. The proximity of those early Christians to Jesus and his apostles and the foundational nature of their work for future generations grant them a singular place in church history.

Evidence for the early Christian's position on abortion is conclusive, but relating that position to problems confronting the modern church is a challenging task. Nevertheless, no historical discussion of abortion would be complete without attempting to interpret the significance of the conclusions reached by Christ's followers in the ancient world for Christ's followers today.

Evaluating the Early Church

In his introduction to *The Early Christian Attitude to War*, C. J. Cadoux cautions:

> The example of our Christian forefathers indeed can never be of itself a sufficient basis for the settlement of our own conduct to-day: the very variations of that example would make such dependence impossible. At the same time the solution of our own ethical problems will involve a study of the mind of Christendom on this same or similar questions during bygone generations: and, for this purpose, perhaps no period of Christian history is so important as that of the first three centuries.[2]

Interpreting church history, then, calls for guidelines for evaluating and applying beliefs and practices of Christians of the past to today's situations. The following four tests may assist this process.

1. *Is the historical belief or practice based on Scripture?* For Christians, ancient beliefs must reflect the gospel of Jesus Christ if they are to be accepted today. Christ, as attested in Scripture, is the final authority in matters of faith and life. Anything which explicitly contradicts the teachings of Scripture cannot be adhered to. If, however, the Bible fails to mention a subject explicitly or to develop its ethical implications, that subject must be studied in light of the general structures of biblical thought. The belief or practice must accord with the implicit corollaries of these general structures.

2. *Does the belief or practice stand the test of universality?* A truly Christian position will not remain limited to one geographical region. It will either spread by natural means or undergo "spontaneous generation" in various places. Specific manifesta-

tions will vary from place to place, but general principles will not.

3. *Does the belief or practice stand the test of time?* Of course, errors can continue and have endured for centuries, but anything truly Christian must last longer than the many short-lived movements which every generation witnesses.

4. *Is the past situation somehow analogous to the contemporary situation?* Minimizing the differences between eras can be dangerous, but examining both similarities and differences is necessary and helpful. Points of contact between past and present free the past to speak to the present, and differences between then and now allow the past to speak on its own terms.

The first and fourth questions are matters of interpretation; the second and third, matters of history. The tests of universality and time reveal that during the first five centuries (and until quite recently) abortion was rejected by Christians everywhere. The test of analogy shows many parallels between the situation faced by early Christians and that of today. Though more sophisticated and safer, today's abortion methods are basically similar to those of two thousand years ago. The practice is undeniably widespread, appearing even in the church. Convenience and concealment of sexual immorality are still frequent motives, though the issue of "the quality of life" has perhaps raised new questions. At the center of the discussion remains the forever debated question of the beginning of human life.

Evaluating the early church's stand on abortion, then, consists mostly of deciding if it reflects the teachings of Scripture and the gospel of Jesus Christ. One way of approaching this process of evaluation is to study the strengths and weaknesses of the traditional Christian view.

A strength of the Christian view was its firm grounding in creation theology such as that expressed in Psalm 139. This theology emphasizes God's bringing about and caring for each individual human being. Another strong foundation of the early church's position was its gospel ethic of love, nonviolence, justice and peace, accompanied at first by a rejection of all violence. This was a consistent ethic of respect for life. Another strength in the earliest period was the absence of legalism either of attitude or of penalties. At the same time, Christians did not issue a license for unbridled liberty. Instead, abortion for them was a personal and social ill needing the redeeming love and influence of God in Christ for its correction.

A weakness in the position of the early Christians was their apparent preoccupation with conviction and condemnation to the near exclusion of compassion and forgiveness. The absence of an *explicit* record of Christian action to relieve the suffering of women in difficult circumstances or to provide for illegitimate children is troubling.[3] Judgment substituting for aid later led to extreme legal punishments. Furthermore, early Christians said little about therapeutic abortion, a topic of importance then as well as today.

On the whole, however, the consistency and inherent logic of the early church's position merit the consideration even of those who do not accept it as normative for today. Grounded in biblical and gospel themes, it functioned as a guide within the Christian community and as a moral influence in the world at large. Even with its deficiencies in the area of compassion and forgiveness, the early Christian attitude toward abortion stands as a unique ethical position in the history of the world.

Contemporary Alternatives

What are the current Christian approaches to the abortion issue, and how do they agree with or differ from the early church's view? Though in reality there is a wide range of opinions, two dominant perspectives now shape non-Christian as well as Christian thinking: "pro-choice" and "pro-life."

The fundamental contention of pro-choice advocates is that abortion is a matter of individual conscience and decision. Of paramount concern is the woman's welfare and right to choose; all other issues are subordinated to this one. Ethical or legal attempts to restrict women's rights are considered unfair. For pro-life advocates abortion is the taking of innocent human life. All other questions are subordinate to one primary ethical issue: the unborn child's welfare and right to live. Ethical and legal restrictions of abortion are therefore seen as both right and good.

Often people who condone abortion, or at least the right to choose, are quick to protest other threats to life such as capital punishment, the nuclear arms build-up and handguns. These pro-choice people often work actively on behalf of the poor and oppressed. Oddly enough, outspoken abortion foes frequently defend the seemingly contradictory causes of capital punishment, the nuclear arms race and relaxed handgun control. The needs and rights of the poor and oppressed often rank low on their agenda of social concerns.[4] This situation has caused many people to ask:

> Will somebody please be consistent about issues of life and death? Where did all the anti-war folks go when the abortion issue came along? And why can't the conservatives who oppose abortion understand the immorality of nuclear weapons?[5]

In face of the threat of nuclear holocaust, many Christians are once again listening to the early church's words on war, peace and Christian moral responsibility. The early church's witness has persuaded many to become either total pacifists or nuclear pacifists. Since abortion—called by one author "the silent holocaust"—is widespread in our day, it seems appropriate to consider the united voice of the early church on that subject as well.[6] The early church provides a model for a logical, consistent pro-life position, one which opposes violence in any form. The early Christians were both pro-peace and pro-life. Theirs was an ethic of love expressed in peace and justice.

A growing number of people already see reason to oppose both abortion and nuclear weaponry and to support concern both for the poor and for the unborn. These people are aiming for a consistent pro-life stance which supports the right to life of every human being: the unborn child, the hungry infant, the condemned prisoner and the entire human race threatened by nuclear disaster.

In November 1980 *Sojourners* magazine devoted an issue to the subject of abortion. Even without complete knowledge of the early church's fully pro-life perspective, the writers developed a coherent, consistent pro-life position nearly identical in spirit to that of the early church. In a series of articles called "What Does It Mean to Be Pro-Life?" contributors normally identified with political activities against poverty and war, such as Jesse Jackson, Daniel Berrigan and Jim Wallis, spoke out against the violent injustice of abortion. Long-time antiabortion activists pleaded for the rights of the poor and an end to the arms race. The magazine sought reconciliation between opposing sides and compassion toward those who had been victims in one way or another of our society's legitimized oppression and violence. Views similar to those expressed in *Sojourners* are emerging elsewhere, most notably among Roman Catholic bishops. Several pro-peace, pro-life groups have formed.[7]

Some people will continue to defend abortion and reject war or nuclear weapons, or vice versa. As they consider the early church they will hear one side of its ethic but not the other. Such positions are indeed theoretically permissible. The early Christians may have been right on one count but not on the other, and what was correct then about one issue may not be correct today. Those who listen to one voice without listening to the other, however, are perhaps unwilling to let the early church speak on its own terms. The early church furnishes a Christian paradigm for avoiding and opposing abortion, war and any other affront to the sanctity of human life. Modern Christians trying to extend their convictions into society by rational persuasion and a consistent witness of belief and practice should carefully consider the model provided by the early church.

From the perspective of the early Christians, a\
tion which opposes abortion but supports the proc\
of violent weapons—especially those intended to ....ocent
people—would be logically inconsistent and fundamentally unchristian.[8] Likewise, a stand which opposes the deployment of
violent weapons but allows or encourages the taking of an unborn's life would be no less inconsistent and unchristian. In
other words the early church would denounce equally the con-
servatives' antiabortion, pro-nuclear weapons position and the
pro-peace, pro-choice (sometimes meaning pro-abortion) position of many large Protestant denominations and organizations.

Toward an Ethic on Behalf of the Unborn

What, then, is the significance of the early church's position
against abortion for today's complex decisions? Early Christian
literature is permeated with themes which could serve as start-
ing points for developing a new ethic on behalf of the unborn.

Creation. Human life is created and sustained by God from
beginning to end. Affirming the fetus as human life, God's
handiwork in the womb, requires no ancient theory of ensoulment but is the response of faith to God's providence. Psalm 139,
an example of such faith, is all the more relevant in a day when
prenatal development can be chronicled by camera.

Incarnation. "The Scriptural affirmation that Jesus was conceived by the Holy Spirit is not without significance (Matthew
1:20; Luke 1:35). For Jesus to become incarnate, to become truly
human, entailed his participation in the full range of human
experience—from conception through death."[9] Jesus' humility
in the Incarnation sanctified and dignified not only humanity as
a whole but also the unborn child. Every conception and every
pregnancy is a unique, unrepeatable event.

Neighbor love. By raising the fetus to the status of neighbor,
Christianity introduces a moral responsibility to the unborn,
who must be treated with the same kind of self-denying, sacri-
ficial love as other human beings.

Enemy love. Jesus explicitly elevated the enemy to the place of neighbor. The enemy must also be treated with self-denying, nonretaliatory love. If an unwanted pregnancy engenders feelings of hatred toward the newly conceived unborn, the gospel supplies the power to transform hatred into love, to consider the fetus not as an enemy to be destroyed but as a neighbor to be loved.

Peace. Christian refusal to support abortion should manifest an attitude of nonviolence. Peacemaking demands removing all forms of hostility toward others, including the unborn.

Justice. The biblical concept of justice involves defending the rights and providing for the needs of the helpless, the innocent and the poor. Unborn children, nearly one-third of whom are aborted each year in the United States, need people to come to their aid and defense.

Even themes that first appear to concern only the twentieth century find parallels in Greco-Roman society.

Liberation. Opposing abortion effects liberation in two senses. First, it liberates unborn children from violence (a concern of the early Christian church). Second, it liberates women from convenient violence committed against their bodies (a problem for women in antiquity, who were often forced to abort). As one feminist has said of a similar situation today:

> We [women] must at least begin to see that abortion, convenient as it is for a woman's "problem," is often more convenient for the lover, or boss, or husband, or father of that woman. Our own liberation must not be based on destroying our children, but on reaching out to our brothers, offering them the word of life, and insisting that they begin to assume their responsibility.[10]

Quality of life. This recent term represents an ancient concept which allowed the Romans, for instance, to expose deformed babies. For Christians to reintroduce distinctions between human lives is a serious error. Christ has removed all such differentiations, destroyed the hierarchy of the relative value of different kinds of people and made all people neighbors. Similarly, as Basil wisely recognized long ago, making arbitrary distinctions between stages of fetal development to permit abortions is inconsistent with Christlike love.[11] The born and unborn, viable and nonviable, the "normal" and the "abnormal" are all of value from a Christian perspective.

Freedom, conscience and rights. The call by pro-choice groups for freedom reflects not a responsible Christian attitude toward freedom but a secularly informed libertinism. Christian freedom can never be made an excuse or cover for sin; rather, it is the process of being transferred out of slavery to sin into the freedom of obedience (Rom 6:16-19). Claims to individual freedom of conscience are no substitute for conformity to the will of God. The plea for abortion rights in the name of women's rights is likewise misguided. In the interest of granting rights, ancient Roman society gave the father absolute power of life and death over his household: wife, servants and children, born and unborn. Today absolute power over the life and death of the fetus is often transferred from the father to the mother. Those who legitimately struggle for women's rights must beware of accepting any rights which prevent the basic right to life of other, though yet unborn, human beings.

These themes are not exhaustive; neither are they fully or finally defined. They merely begin to address the need of forming a Christian ethic for the unborn, a problem which merits much further study.

The early church's belief and practice challenge contemporary Christians to three responses. First, Christians must engage in reflection. The original vision of the early church should be a major focus of study as modern Christians strive for a unified position, a resolution to the present dichotomy. Until the safety of each individual, born or unborn, is secured, concern for the preservation of the race has little meaning. Until efforts are made to preserve the human race from nuclear war, concern for the safety of the unborn may prove to be in vain. No survivors of a nuclear war could possibly suffer greater harm than unborn children.

Second, Christians need to plan and prepare for a united effort in the name of Christ to end the silent holocaust and to prevent a nuclear holocaust. Creative alternatives to each form of violence and oppression need to be considered and then organized. Progress may already be seen in groups and individuals who care for women with unwanted pregnancies or adopt unwanted children of women who decide against abortion, and in those who are working to develop a peace academy and other alternatives to violence. Until our society sees viable alternatives to present practices, no changes will occur.[12]

Finally, Christians need to allow their personal beliefs to shape their political and social involvement. Many keep their beliefs to themselves, not wishing to force personal convictions on others. Of course, forcing one's opinion on another is neither wise nor Christian, but Christians may rightly attempt persuasion. Agreeing to a political view simply for the sake of avoiding conflict with society is not the Christian way. It is just as inconsistent to believe abortion is wrong and then to support a pro-choice position as it would be to believe nuclear weapons are sinful and then to allow each government the option of using them or not. Whatever specific political actions Christians take, they should function on the side of life and peace.

In all these responses, Christians are called to speak and act from a position of humble service rather than self-righteous power. Above all, to those who have had or performed abortions must go forth a word of compassion, forgiveness and new life in Christ. Similarly, to those guilty of militarism and other forms of violence, a promise of personal and corporate renewal must be offered as well as a pronouncement of judgment and a call to repentance.

If the early church is allowed to speak, it will plead with Christians today to abstain from all manifestations of bloodshed and violence, especially the two major forms facing us today: abortion and the nuclear arms race. It will also urge Christians to work to reduce these in their society and world. Clearly the love of Christ channeled through his followers is powerful enough to guide the church and the world toward a consistent affirmation of life.

NOTES

Chapter 1: Abortion in the Ancient World

[1]Juvenal *Satire* 6. 592-601.

[2]Ibid.

[3]Soranos *Gynecology* 1. 19, cited in John T. Noonan, Jr., *Contraception: A History of Its Treatment by the Catholic Theologians and Canonists* (Cambridge, Mass.: Belknap Press, 1965), p. 18; Suetonius *Domitian* 22; Juvenal *Satire* 6. 592-601; Clement of Alexandria *Paedagogus* 2. 10. 96. 1; Origen *Against Heresies* 9; Hippolytus *Refutation of All Heresies* 9. 7; *Apocalypse of Peter* (Ethiopic text); Jerome *Letter* 22. 13; Synod of Elvira, Canon 68; Synod of Ancyra, Canon 21; Chrysostom *Homily* 24 on Romans.

[4]Juvenal *Satire* 6. 592-601. See also Soranos *Gynecology* 1. 19, cited in Noonan, *Contraception*, p. 18.

[5]Chrysostom *Homily* 24 on Romans. Cf. Soranos *Gynecology* 1. 19, cited in John T. Noonan, Jr., "An Almost Absolute Value in History," in *The Morality of Abortion: Legal and Historical Perspectives*, ed. John T. Noonan, Jr. (Cambridge, Mass.: Belknap Press, 1970), p. 4.

[6]Plato *Republic* 5. 9 and Aristotle *Politics* 7. 14. 10; Will Durant, *Caesar and Christ* (New York: Simon and Schuster, 1944), pp. 665-66; Noonan, *Contraception*, pp. 20-24; and Tacitus *Annals* 3. 25.

[7]Ambrose *Hexameron* 5. 18. 58; Hippolytus *Refutation of All Heresies* 9. 7.

[8]Justinian *Digest* 48. 19. 39.

[9]Epiphanius *Panarion*, cited in John A. Hardon, "Euthanasia and Abortion: A Catholic View," *Human Life Review* 1, no. 4 (Fall 1975):96-97.

[10]Soranos *Gynecology* 1. 19, cited in Noonan, *Contraception*, p. 18.

[11]They are mentioned by Hippocrates, Ovid, Soranos, Juvenal, Clement of Alexandria, M. Felix, Justinian *Digest*, Jerome, Basil, Ambrose and others.

[12]Soranos, cited in John A. Rasmussen, "Abortion: Historical and Biblical Perspectives," *Concordia Theological Quarterly* 43, no. 1 (January 1979):19. See Celsus *De medicina* 5. 21. 5 for examples. Hippocrates *Oath* condemns the dispensing of an abortive pessary, *pesson phthorion.*

[13]Galen *On the Natural Faculties* 3. 12. 184.

[14]Noonan, *Contraception*, pp. 13-14. Cf. Ovid *Heroides* 11. 33-42.

[15]Celsus *De medicina* 5. 35. 13.

[16]Pliny *Natural History* 20. 22; 21. 18; 24. 16; 7. 7; 28. 19. In a series of strange pregnancy-related myths in 7. 6. 42, Pliny states that a sneeze after intercourse causes abortion.

[17]Soranos himself confirms these two points in *Gynecology* 1. 19, cited in Noonan, *Contraception*, pp. 14, 17.

[18]J. H. Waszink, "Abtreibung," *Reallexikon für Antike und Christentum* (Stuttgart: Hiersemann Verlag, 1950), 1:58.

[19]Ovid *Fasti* 1. 621-24; Hippolytus *Refutation of All Heresies* 9. 7; Origen *Against Heresies* 9.

[20]Tertullian *De anima* 25.

[21]Celsus *De medicina* 7. 29. Augustine *Enchiridion* 86 mentions a procedure of cutting away limb by limb for the same problem.

[22]Pliny *Natural History* 7. 6; 7. 5. 40. Pregnancy was believed to be detectable by the woman on day ten by the symptoms of headache, giddiness, dim sight, distaste for food, and vomiting.

Chapter 2: The Pagan World

[1]Harold O. J. Brown, "What the Supreme Court Didn't Know," *Human Life Review* 1, no. 2 (Spring 1975):11; Roger Huser, *Crime of Abortion in Canon Law* (Washington: Catholic University Press, 1942), p. 4.

[2]Brown, "Supreme Court," p. 12, notes that many modern authors doubt the existence of antiabortion codes in ancient Greece, while Huser, *Canon Law*, p. 4, and Waszink, "Abtreibung," col. 56, suggest that such codes continued from the time of Lycurgus and Solon. R. Crahay, "Les Moralistes Anciens et l'Avortement," *L'Antiquité Classique* 10 (1941):11-12, argues that pseudo-Galen simply misinterpreted a story about Lycurgus in Plutarch *Lycurgus* 3 in which the lawgiver opposes the abortion of the fetus of his brother's (the king's) widow, in order to spare her danger, and counsels exposure instead. In reality Lycurgus had no intention of exposing the child, but the story reveals more about Lycurgus's respect for his brother than about his ideas on abortion or exposure. Crahay, however, does not prove that pseudo-Galen's claims rest on this story.

[3]Musonius Rufus *Discourse* 15 in Cora E. Lutz, *Musonius Rufus: The Roman Socrates* (New Haven: Yale University Press, 1947), p. 97. A. C. van Geyten-beek, *Musonius Rufus and Greek Diatribe* (Assen: Van Gorcum, 1963), pp. 78-79, n. 1, argues that the reference is to the Augustan reforms and not to ancient laws.

[4]On exposure in ancient Greece see Aristotle *Politics* 2. 6; 7. 16; Plato *Republic* 5; A. Cameron, "The Exposure of Children and Greek Ethics," *The Classical Review* 46, no. 3 (July 1932):105-14.

[5]Egyptian laws are mentioned in Aelian *Variae Historiae* 2. 7. Their relationship to Greek law is discussed by Franz Dölger, "Das Lebensrecht des ungeborenen Kindes und die Fruchtabtreibung in der Bewertung der heidnischen und christlichen Antike," in *Antike und Christentum*, Band IV (Münster: Aschendorffsche Verlagsbuchhandlung, 1934), pp. 14-15.

[6]Hippocrates, *Works*, 3 vols., Loeb Classical Library (London, 1923-27), 1: 291-92.

[7]Huser, *Canon Law*, pp. 4-5, especially n. 12.

[8]See Cameron, "Exposure," p. 110, and Waszink, "Abtreibung," 57.

[9]Brown, "Supreme Court," pp. 12-13.

[10]Huser, *Canon Law*, pp. 4-5.

[11]Plato *Republic* 5.9.

[12]Plutarch *De placitis philosophorum* 5. 15.

[13]This point is made by Waszink, "Abtreibung," 56, and Crahay, "Les Moralistes," p. 23.

[14]Aristotle *Politics* 7. 1. 1.

[15]Aristotle *Politics* 7. 14. 10.

[16]Aristotle *Historia animalium* 7. 3.

[17]Hardon, "Euthanasia and Abortion," p. 93. See also Dölger, "Das Lebensrecht," p. 21.

[18]Musonius Rufus *Discourse* 15.

[19]Hardon, "Euthanasia and Abortion," p. 93.

[20]Orphic concern for the unborn is noted by Waszink, "Abtreibung," col. 55. For Orphic influence on Stoicism, see Cameron, "Exposure," pp. 109-11.

[21]Dölger, "Das Lebensrecht," pp. 15-20; Waszink, "Abtreibung," 56; Cameron, "Exposure," p. 108; Crahay, "Les Moralistes," pp. 16-17. These inscriptions date from several centuries before Christ to several centuries after.

[22]Plutarch *Lives, Romulus* 22. 3. The word he used was *pharmakeia*.

[23]Theodor Mommsen, *Römisches Strafrecht* (Leipzig: Duncker and Humblot, 1899), p. 636.

[24]Waszink, "Abtreibung," col. 57, claims that the whole report is uncertain, but Mommsen, *Römisches Strafrecht*, p. 636, accepts it as a valid record of ancient law.

[25]Durant, *Caesar and Christ*, p. 57, and H. Bennett, "The Exposure of Infants in Ancient Rome," *The Classical Journal* 18 (1922-23):342. Cf. Cicero *De legibus* 3. 8.

[26]Germain G. Grisez, *Abortion: The Myths, the Realities, and the Arguments* (New York: Corpus Books, 1970), p. 185.

[27]Justinian *Digest* 48. 8. 8.

[28]Justinian *Digest* 35. 2. 9. 1; 25. 4. 1. 1. This was also the view of Alexandrian philosophers and physicians, according to Philo *Special Laws* 3. 20. 117.

[29]The problem in the application of *Lex Cornelia* to abortion is that the evidence both for the Roman legal view of the fetus and for the banishment of women who had aborted is in Justinian's sixth-century A.D. *Digest*. Although the *Digest* preserves older legal works which in turn preserve ancient custom, one cannot be sure that even second- and third-century interpretations are accurate. Huser, *Canon Law*, p. 9, and Grisez, *Abortion*, pp. 185-86, think that *Lex Cornelia* was applied to abortion; Noonan, *Contraception*, p. 26, argues that it was not; and Mommsen, *Römisches Strafrecht*, p. 637, implies that it was not.

[30]Cicero *Pro Cluentio* 11. 32. Grisez, *Abortion*, pp. 185-86, suggests that the real reason for the Milesian woman's death was that she was not a free woman and aborted without her husband's permission. Cicero's point, however, is the correctness of her being put to death for having an abortion.

[31]Durant, *Caesar and Christ*, p. 222.

[32]Brown, "Supreme Court," p. 14.

[33]Noonan, *Contraception*, p. 21.

[34]Grisez, *Abortion*, p. 186, and Waszink, "Abtreibung," col. 57.

[35]Seneca *De ira* 1. 15, cited in Hardon, "Euthanasia and Abortion," p. 93, and Tertullian *Apology* 29. 27.

[36]Durant, *Caesar and Christ*, p. 313.

[37]Seneca *To Helvia on Consolation* 16. 3.

[38]Suetonius *Domitian* 22; Juvenal *Satire* 2. 29-35.

[39]E.g., *Heroides* 11. 33-42.

[40]Ovid *Metamorphoses* 8. Similarly, *Amores* 2. 14. 5-6.

[41]*Amores* 2. 14. 1-8.

[42]*Metamorphoses* 8.

[43]Ovid *De nuce*, lines 22-23, cited in William H. L. Lecky, *History of European Morals from Augustus to Charlemagne*, vol. 2 (New York: D. Appleton and Company, 1872), p. 23. Cf. *Amores* 2. 13 concerning another (probably fictitious) mistress.

[44]In Aulus Gellius *Noctes Atticae* 12. 1, cited in Lecky, *European Morals*, 2:23.

[45]Juvenal *Satire* 6. 592-601. Latin *homines in ventro necandos*, from *necare*, "to put to death, usually by violent means."

[46]Noonan, *Contraception*, p. 18.

[47]Ibid.; and Soranos *Gynecology* 3. 19. 60, cited in Brown, "Supreme Court," p. 14.

[48]See Geytenbeek, *Musonius Rufus*, pp. 3-50, and Lutz, *Musonius Rufus*, pp. 3-30.

[49]Lutz, *Musonius Rufus*, pp. 3-4, 14-17; and Geytenbeek, *Musonius Rufus*, pp. 3-4.

[50]*Discourse* 13 A and B, in Lutz, *Musonius Rufus*.

[51]*Discourse* 12.

[52]*Discourse* 15. Geytenbeek, *Musonius Rufus*, pp. 78-79, n. 1, explains the mention of laws as a reference to the Augustan reforms.

[53]See Crahay, "Les Moralistes," pp. 16-17.

[54]Mommsen, *Römisches Strafrecht*, p. 637.

[55]Justinian *Digest* 47. 11; see also Huser, *Canon Law*, p. 9, n. 34; and Grisez, *Abortion*, p. 186.

[56]Justinian *Digest* 48. 8. 8. Ulpian did not specify the length of banishment. Although the text makes it sound permanent, the penalty was more likely similar in length to that prescribed by Septimus and Antoninus.

[57]Justinian *Digest* 48. 19. 39.

[58]Justinian *Digest* 48. 19. 38. 5.

[59]Noonan, *Contraception*, p. 27, thinks the interpretation began in the second century.

[60]It is possible, though unlikely, that third-century legislation embodied customs or statutes dating from the late first or second centuries A.D.

[61]Huser, *Canon Law*, p. 11.

[62]So also Noonan, *Contraception*, p. 86.

[63]Justinian *Digest* 35. 2. 9. 1. Papinian's friendship with Septimus may have influenced the latter's prescript on abortion.

[64]Justinian *Digest* 25. 4. 1. 1; 38. 8. 1. 8. Cf. Mommsen, *Römisches Strafrecht*, p. 636, n. 5, and Huser, *Canon Law*, p. 10.

[65]Justinian *Digest* 37. 9. 1. 15.

Chapter 3: The Jewish World

[1]Exodus 21:22-23 contains legal provisions only for accidental abortion. Similar is the *Code of Hammurabi* (ca 1800 B.C.), whereas the *Sumerian Code* (ca 2000 B.C.) speaks also of a deliberate attack on a pregnant woman, and the *Assyrian Code* (ca 1500 B.C.) and the Persian *Vendidad* (ca 600 B.C.) condemn deliberate abortion per se. See Huser, *Canon Law*, pp. 2-4.

[2]Hecataeus of Abdera, in Menaham Stone, ed., *Greek and Latin Authors on Jews and Judaism*, 2 vols. (Jerusalem: Israel Academy of Sciences and Humanities, 1974-80), 1:33; Tacitus *Histories* 5. 3; Babylonian Talmud (hereafter TB) *Yebamoth* 63b. (The Mishnah will be indicated simply by the name of the tractate.)

[3]See (1) Genesis 1:28; TB *Yebamoth* 63b; (2) Genesis 1; Psalm 139; TB *Niddah* 31a; (3) Leviticus 17; Acts 15; Mishnah and TB *Kerithoth* and *Niddah*.

[4]This was first carefully worked out by V. Aptowitzer, "Observations on the Criminal Law of the Jews," *Jewish Quarterly Review* 15 (1924):55-118. It is followed by David Feldman, *Birth Control in Jewish Law* (New York: New York University Press, 1968), pp. 257-60, and Huser, *Canon Law*, pp. 5-8.

[5]Aptowitzer, "Observations," pp. 88, 115-16.

[6]My translation. See Feldman, *Birth Control*, p. 257.

[7]Aptowitzer, "Observations," pp. 115-16.

[8]See Huser, *Canon Law*, pp. 6-7.

[9]Philo *Special Laws* 3. 108-9.

[10]Philo *Special Laws* 3. 117.

[11]*Sentences of Pseudo-Phocylides* 184-85.

[12]For a detailed discussion of this writer, see P. W. van der Horst, *The Sentences of Pseudo-Phocylides, with Introduction and Commentary*, vol. 4 in *Studia in Veteris Testamenti Pseudepigrapha*, ed. A. M. Denis and M. de Jonge (Leiden: E. J. Brill, 1978), especially pp. 232-35. He suggests that line 186, "Lay not your hand upon your wife when she is pregnant," is probably a paraphrase of the Septuagint of Exodus 21:22, although it may rather refer to sexual intercourse. The *Sentences of Pseudo-Phocylides* exalt procreation in lines 175-76.

[13]*Sibylline Oracles* 2. 339-42, trans. Milton S. Terry (New York: Hunt and Eaton, 1890). Book 3. 909-10 may include abortion in its condemnation of infanticide. Other editions of the *Oracles* number these references as 2. 281 and 3. 765, respectively.

[14]This association of abortion with both sexual immorality and social injustice will have parallels in Christian writings.

[15]Feldman, *Birth Control*, p. 284.

[16]Aptowitzer, "Observations," pp. 115-16; TB *Niddah* 22b-23a.

[17]TB *Sanhedrin* 91b.

[18]TB *Sanhedrin* 110b.

[19]So also Feldman, *Birth Control*, pp. 271-75, *contra* Aptowitzer, "Observations,"

pp. 68-75, 85-118.

[20]*Niddah* 3. 7 and TB *Niddah* 30b.

[21]*Niddah* 3. 2-3; cf. TB *Niddah* 24b-25b.

[22]A secondary concern was to determine the inheritance rights and duties of the first-born son whose identity and status depended on the legal interpretation of his mother's previous miscarriage(s). See *Niddah* 3. 2-3, 6-7; TB *Niddah* 23b-26a; *Kerithoth* 1. 3-6; *Bekhoroth* 8. 1.

[23]*Niddah* 5. 1.

[24]Josephus *Antiquities* 4. 278; see also TB *Sanhedrin* 74a and 79a and *Baba Kamma* 5. 4 for similar understandings of Exodus.

[25]TB *Hullin* 58a; Rabbi Judah in TB *Gittin* 23b; TB *Niddah* 44a; TB *Baba Batra* 142a; cf. *Niddah* 5. 3; TB *Niddah* 43b-44b; TB *Arakin* 7a-b; see also Aptowitzer, "Observations," p. 90. Samuel Belkin, *Philo and the Oral Law* (Cambridge, Mass.: Harvard University Press, 1940), pp. 131-39, maintains that the rabbis generally considered the fetus legally a person, but he examines only the evidence which supports his thesis.

[26]*Oholoth* 7. 6. This idea was debated among the rabbis.

[27]See Feldman, *Birth Control*, pp. 275, 284.

[28]Feldman, *Birth Control*, p. 254.

[29]TB *Niddah* 31a. The scriptural reference is to Psalm 139:13-14.

[30]TB *Yebamoth* 63b-64a.

[31]Josephus *Against Apion* 2. 202.

[32]*Yebamoth* 7. 4; TB *Baba Batra* 141b-142a; TB *Hullin* 72a. See Aptowitzer, "Observations," pp. 69-75, for texts.

[33]Feldman, *Birth Control*, pp. 259, 261.

[34]TB *Sanhedrin* 57b. Curiously, this condemnation of abortion as murder (for non-Jews) remained part of Jewish law. See Feldman, *Birth Control*, pp. 259-60.

[35]See Aptowitzer, "Observations," pp. 113-14, and Feldman, *Birth Control*, pp. 259-60, for this and other suggestions on the source of this law.

[36]This is the position of Aptowitzer, Feldman and Huser.

Chapter 4: Christian Beginnings: The First Three Centuries

[1]Paul's use of *ektrōma* in 1 Corinthians 15:8 may refer to abortion, but the usage is enigmatic.

[2]See H. G. Liddell and R. Scott, *A Greek-English Lexicon*, revised and augmented by H. S. Jones *et al.* (Oxford: Clarendon Press, 1968).

[3]Soranos *Gynecology* 1. 59.

[4]Waszink, "Abtreibung," 59, states that it is "very likely" that these texts include condemnation of abortion.

[5]John A. T. Robinson, *Redating the New Testament* (Philadelphia: Westminster Press, 1976), pp. 312-35, argues for a mid to late first-century date for both the *Didache* and the *Epistle of Barnabas*.

[6]Athanasius *Festal Letter* 39. That Athanasius's reference to "teaching of [the] apostles" refers to the *Didache* itself is held by Johannes Quasten, *Patrology*, vol. 1: *The Beginnings of Patristic Literature*; vol. 2: *The Ante-Nicene Litera-*

ture after Irenaeus; vol. 3: *The Golden Age of Greek Patristic Literature;* 3 vols. (Utrecht and Antwerp: Spectrum Publishers, 1950-60), 1:37. L. W. Barnard, *Studies in the Apostolic Fathers and Their Background* (Oxford: Basil Blackwell, 1966), pp. 87-107, contends that the "Two Ways" theme in a separate document was known throughout the early Church and is the subject of Athanasius's reference here.

[7]*Didache* 1. 1.

[8]*Didache* 2. 2.

[9]*Ou phoneuseis teknon en phthora.* That *phthora,* "destruction," refers to abortion, not infanticide, is clear from the following: *oude gennēthen apokteneis.*

[10]*Epistle of Barnabas* 19. 5.

[11]Noonan, "Absolute Value," p. 10, contends that even therapeutic abortion is rejected by this joining of the abortion prohibition and the command to love one's neighbor above oneself.

[12]*Didache* 5. 1-2. The words are *phoneis teknōn.*

[13]*Didache* 5. 2. The phrase is *phthoreis plasmatos theou.*

[14]Ms. L of the *Didache* dates from the eleventh century but transmits a third-century translation, according to Quasten, *Patrology,* 1:37-38. On *phthoreus,* see Liddell and Scott, *Lexicon,* and Walter Bauer, *A Greek-English Lexicon of the New Testament and Other Early Christian Literature,* 2d English ed., revised and augmented by F. Wilbur Gingrich and Frederick W. Danker (Chicago: The University of Chicago Press, 1979).

[15]*Epistle of Barnabas* 20. 1-2.

[16]The absence of the formed/unformed distinction makes it difficult to contend that this condemnation comes from the Septuagint or Alexandrian Christianity *alone,* as does Aptowitzer, "Observations," p. 85. As we saw in the previous chapter, deliberate abortion was implicitly condemned even in Palestinian thought. This is further confirmed by the fact that the "Two Ways" tradition was not unique to Alexandria but was found in places such as Syria, according to Barnard, *Studies,* pp. 87-107.

[17]Quasten, *Patrology,* 1:144.

[18]*Apocalypse of Peter* 26, the *Akhmim Fragment,* in Edgar Hennecke, *New Testament Apocrypha,* ed. Wilhelm Schneemelcher, English ed. R. McL. Wilson, 2 vols. (Philadelphia: Westminster Press, 1963-65), 2:674. Cameron, "Exposure," p. 111, thinks that the infants in the scene, as in the Orphic tradition, are condemned because they are in the same place as their mothers. But it is more likely that their presence is an apocalyptic literary device to express vividly the wrath of God toward the mothers, and that the infants' salvation is implicit.

[19]*Apocalypse of Peter* 21-34.

[20]The Ethiopic text, in Hennecke-Schneemelcher, *Apocrypha,* 2:674. Although the text could be referring to the case of infanticide described immediately before, Clement of Alexandria understood it to refer to both infanticide and abortion, described just before infanticide. Clement of Alexandria *Prophetic Eclogues* 41 and 48-49, quoted in *Apocrypha,* 2:674-75.

[21]Clement of Alexandria *Prophetic Eclogues* 41 and 48-49, quoted in Hennecke-Schneemelcher, *Apocrypha*, 2:674-75.

[22]See Dölger, "Das Lebensrecht," pp. 28-32. Dölger thinks that this writer was probably a Platonist, deriving his ideas from Plato's doctrine of the fetus as a living being.

[23]The role of angels is different but no less important in the *Apocalypse of Peter*. The connection of angels with conception here seems also to have influenced Origen, according to Dölger, "Das Lebensrecht," pp. 31-32.

[24]As we will see, especially Tertullian *De anima* 26. 4 and Chrysostom *Homily 24 on the Epistle to the Romans*.

[25]Clement of Alexandria *Paedagogus* 1. 1. 1. 4.

[26]Clement of Alexandria *Paedagogus* 2. 10. 96. 1.

[27]Clement *Prophetical Extracts (Prophetic Eclogues)*, in *The Ante-Nicene Fathers*, ed. Alexander Roberts and James Donaldson, 10 vols. (Grand Rapids, Mich.: Wm. B. Eerdmans, 1951-53), 2:571-80.

[28]Athenagoras *Legatio* 35. The lines not quoted base a similar argument on exposure.

[29]Tertullian *Apology* 7. 1.

[30]Tertullian *Apology* 9. 1.

[31]Tertullian *Apology* 9. 6.

[32]Philo *Special Laws* 3. 19. 109.

[33]Tertullian *De anima* 25. 3.

[34]See Quasten, *Patrology*, 2:289.

[35]*De anima* 26. 4.

[36]*De anima* 26. 5.

[37]*De anima* 25. 4-5. Tertullian's reference to therapeutic abortion is not an argument for his acceptance of it, as Dölger, "Das Lebensrecht," pp. 45-49, contends, but is merely one of several examples he uses to prove that the fetus is a living person, for only a living person can be killed and extracted to save the mother.

[38]*De anima* 37. 1.

[39]*De anima* 37. 2.

[40]Brown, "Supreme Court," p. 9, argues that *forma* means here "essential character," not physical form, but this interpretation disregards the context of the passage.

[41]Tertullian concludes chapter 36 with this statement about Eve: "So for a certain length of time her flesh was without specific form, such as she had when taken from Adam's side; but she was then herself, a living being, since I would then consider her soul as a part of Adam. Besides, God's breath would have given her life, if she had not received both soul and body from Adam."

[42]Papinian, in Justinian *Digest* 35. 2. 9. 1, records the Roman law.

[43]Minucius Felix *Octavius* 30. 1-6.

[44]Minucius Felix *Octavius* 30. 2.

[45]Minucius Felix *Octavius* 30. 6.

[46]Origen *Against Heresies* 9; cf. Hippolytus *Refutation of All Heresies* 9. 7; Cyprian

Letter 48.

[47]Origen *Homily* 10, "On the pregnant woman whom two men, while fighting, cause to abort." His *Hexapla* lists *yeladēyah*, *progenies ejus*, *to paidion*, and *embryon* as names for what was aborted according to Exodus 21:22.

[48]Hippolytus *Refutation of All Heresies (Philosophumena)* 9. 7. See the discussion in Dölger, "Das Lebensrecht," pp. 43-44.

[49]Cyprian *Letter* 52. 2 (numbered 48 in some editions). "The fruit of a father's murder" probably refers to the aborted child, although another possible translation, "quickly after a parricide" (Sister Rose Barnard Donna in *The Fathers of the Church: A New Translation* [Washington, D.C.: Catholic University of America Press, 1964], p. 129) would relate this event to Novatian's just-previous failure to bury his dead father. However, since Novatian did not cause his father's death, the murder referred to must be that of the aborted infant, as the *Ante-Nicene Fathers* text quoted would suggest.

[50]Cited in Hennecke-Scheemelcher, *Apocrypha*, 2:675.

[51]Ibid., 2:784-85.

[52]Justinian *Digest* 47. 11. 4; 48. 8; 48. 19. 38-39.

[53]R. M. Grant, *Augustus to Constantine* (New York: Harper and Row, 1970), p. 272. On pp. 97-99 Grant also notes that Septimus Severus was quite favorable to Christians according to Tertullian, and argues that the emperor's supposed edict of ca 202 forbidding Jews and Christians on pain of death to make converts did not really exist. If Grant is correct, the possibility of Christian influence on the emperor is increased. If he is incorrect, it is still possible that Septimus Severus was affected by Christian ethics even though he did not convert or wish others to abandon the Roman gods.

Chapter 5: Christianity Established: The Fourth and Fifth Centuries

[1]Epiphanius *Panarion*, cited in Hardon, "Euthanasia and Abortion," pp. 96-97.

[2]Charles Joseph Hefele, *A History of the Christian Councils*, vol. 1: *To the Close of the Council of Nicaea*, trans. and ed. William R. Clark (Edinburgh: T. & T. Clark, 1871), pp. 131-72.

[3]The Latin *communio* may refer either to the Eucharist or perhaps to absolution, according to Huser, *Canon Law*, p. 18.

[4]Text in Hefele, *Nicaea*, p. 164. See also Dölger, "Das Lebensrecht," pp. 54-57.

[5]Huser, *Canon Law*, p. 17.

[6]Ibid., p. 19.

[7]Ephraem *De timore Dei* 10, cited in Brown, "Supreme Court," p. 16.

[8]Text in Hefele, *Nicaea*, p. 220. See also Dölger, "Das Lebensrecht," pp. 54-57.

[9]So Hefele, *Nicaea*, p. 220; but see Huser, *Canon Law*, p. 20, who thinks it refers to an earlier law not otherwise recorded.

[10]*Spoudazō*. See Huser, *Canon Law*, p. 20.

[11]According to Gregory of Nazianzus, *Orat.* 43. 66, cited in Quasten, *Patrology*, 3:208.

[12]Basil *Letter* 188. 2.

[13]Basil had also recommended ten years for involuntary murder and twenty for

willful murder. Since he obviously viewed abortion as willful murder, according to this letter, it has been suggested that the element of shame involved in abortion led to his reduction of the sentence to ten years. See Sister Agnes Clare Way, trans. and ed., in *The Fathers of the Church* series (1955), vol. 28, p. 13, n. 37.

[14]Basil's reference to the danger of death to mothers could easily be dismissed today, but such a dismissal would violate Basil's spirit of moral concern for motives.

[15]Basil *Letter* 188. 2.

[16]Ambrose *Hexameron* 5. 18. 58 (the eighth homily, on day five).

[17]Quoted in Grisez, *Abortion*, p. 143.

[18]T. C. Lawler, ed., *The Letters of St. Jerome*, trans. C. C. Mierow, Ancient Christian Writers, vol. 33 (Westminster, Md.: Newman Press, 1963), p. 3.

[19]Jerome *Letter* 22. 13 (to Eustochium).

[20]Jerome *Letter* 121 (to Algasiam), q. 4, n. 5, cited in Huser, *Canon Law*, p. 16, n. 22.

[21]Latin *canones ecclesiastici apostolorum*.

[22]*Apostolic Constitutions* 7. 3.

[23]Quoting the second-century *phoneis teknōn* and *phthoreis plasmatos theou* (Latin *in abortione corrumpentes creaturam Dei*).

[24]See Huser, *Canon Law*, p. 15; and J. N. D. Kelley, *Early Christian Doctrines*, rev. ed. (New York: Harper and Row, 1978), pp. 345-46.

[25]Augustine *On Marriage and Concupiscence* 1. 1-17.

[26]Augustine *Questiones de Exodo* 9. 80; *Questiones in Heptateucheum* 2.

[27]Augustine *On Marriage and Concupiscence* 1. 17 (15).

[28]Augustine *Enchiridion* 23. 85. 3.

[29]Augustine *Enchiridion* 23. 85. 4.

[30]Augustine *Enchiridion* 23. 86.

[31]Augustine *On Marriage and Concupiscence* 1. 1, written A.D. 419-20.

[32]Chrysostom *Homily 24 on Romans*.

[33]Ibid.

Chapter 6: Abortion and the Early Church: The Wider Context

[1]Dölger, "Das Lebensrecht," pp. 28-32.

[2]Cameron, "Exposure," pp. 109-14.

[3]Feldman, *Birth Control*, pp. 268-71.

[4]Cameron, "Exposure," pp. 110-14.

[5]See Musonius Rufus *Discourses* 12-15, especially 15.

[6]Crahay, "Les Moralistes," pp. 16-17.

[7]Musonius Rufus *Discourse* 13; cf. Noonan, *Contraception*, pp. 46-49, who correctly underscores Stoic emphasis on procreation but neglects the community theme.

[8]Feldman, *Birth Control*, pp. 21-59.

[9]Musonius Rufus *Discourses* 13-14.

[10]Feldman, *Birth Control*, pp. 60-105.

¹¹Ibid., pp. 75-77, 109-226.

¹²See 1 Corinthians 7:1-5; Ephesians 5:22-33.

¹³See Matthew 19:12; 1 Corinthians 7:32-35.

¹⁴On this development see Noonan, *Contraception*, pp. 36-46, 56-85.

¹⁵Ibid., pp. 12-18, 25-27, 44-45, 92.

¹⁶Ibid., pp. 63-68.

¹⁷Ibid., pp. 95-96.

¹⁸Ibid., pp. 107-12.

¹⁹Ibid., pp. 72-84, 91-106.

²⁰Hippolytus *Refutation of All Heresies* 9. 7.

²¹See Noonan, *Contraception*, pp. 93-94.

²²The early Christian ideas about contraception are examined in ibid., pp. 92-102. Noonan, however, often attempts to find references to contraception in places where abortion is the only clear and certain subject discussed.

²³Ibid., pp. 72-81.

²⁴Ibid., p. 91.

²⁵Noonan several times suggests that the Christians' anticontraception stand developed as an extension of their antiabortion position, but he fails to prove any definite progression of this kind in the Christian texts themselves. See ibid., pp. 85-91.

²⁶Tertullian *Apology* 39. 5-7, quoted in Everett Ferguson, *Early Christians Speak: Faith and Life in the First Three Centuries* (Austin, Texas: Sweet Publishing Company, 1971), p. 210.

²⁷Irenaeus *Against Heresies* 4. 14. 3, quoted in Ferguson, *Early Christians Speak*, p. 209.

²⁸Clement of Alexandria *Who Is the Rich Man that Is Saved?* 33-34, quoted in Ferguson, *Early Christians Speak*, p. 209.

²⁹On the three deadly sins see Roland H. Bainton, *Christian Attitudes toward War and Peace* (Nashville: Abingdon Press, 1960), pp. 77-78. On excommunication for murder, see C. John Cadoux, *The Early Christian Attitude to War* (London: Headley Bros. Publishers, Ltd., 1919), p. 57.

³⁰Origen *Contra Celsum* 3. 7, quoted in Jean-Michel Hornus, *It Is Not Lawful for Me to Fight: Early Christian Attitudes toward War, Violence, and the State* (revised edition), trans. Alan Kreider and Oliver Coburn (Scottdale, Pennsylvania: Herald Press, 1980), p. 217.

³¹Tertullian *Apology* 37. 5.

³²Lactantius *Divine Institutions* 6. 20. 10. 15-17, quoted in Hornus, *It Is Not Lawful*, p. 116.

³³Lactantius *Divine Institutions* 6. 20. 10. 15, quoted in Hornus, *It Is Not Lawful*, p. 116. Cf. Athenagoras *Legatio* 35.

³⁴For a concise summary with many insights see Bainton, *Christian Attitudes*, pp. 53-100, especially pp. 66-84, which covers the time between the New Testament and Constantine. A recent thorough study is that of Hornus, *It Is Not Lawful for Me to Fight*. Earlier classic studies include Adolf von Harnack, *Militia Christi* (Tübingen, 1905); Henry J. Cadbury, "The Basis of Early Chris-

tian Anti-Militarism," *Journal of Biblical Literature* 37 (1918):66-94; and C. John Cadoux, *Early Christian Attitude*. A Catholic perspective is provided by William R. Durland, *No King but Caesar? A Catholic Lawyer Looks at Christian Violence* (Scottdale, Pennsylvania: Herald Press, 1975).

[35]Justin *Dialogue with Trypho* 109; 110. 3, quoted in Hornus, *It Is Not Lawful*, p. 85.

[36]Tertullian *On the Crown* 11, quoted in Ferguson, *Early Christians Speak*, p. 220.

[37]Tertullian *On Idolatry* 19, quoted in Ferguson, *Early Christians Speak*, p. 220.

[38]Lactantius *Divine Institutions* 6. 6. 18-24, quoted in Hornus, *It Is Not Lawful*, pp. 114-15.

[39]Tertullian *On the Crown* 12, quoted in Cadoux, *Early Christian Attitude*, p. 113.

[40]Harnack, *Militia Christi*, pp. 46-47.

[41]Bainton, *Christian Attitudes*, p. 74. Tertullian in *On Idolatry* recognizes the difficulty of avoiding idolatry in the army.

[42]Hornus, *It Is Not Lawful*, p. 158; Bainton, *Christian Attitudes*, pp. 79-81.

[43]Tertullian *On the Crown* 11; Hippolytus *Apostolic Tradition* 16. 17-19, both quoted in Ferguson, *Early Christians Speak*, p. 220.

[44]Cadoux, *Early Christian Attitude*, pp. 228-43.

[45]Ibid., pp. 194-211.

[46]Ibid., pp. 242-43.

[47]Bainton, *Christian Attitudes*, pp. 91-100. Hornus, *It Is Not Lawful*, pp. 180-81; Durland, *No King but Caesar?* pp. 90-96.

[48]Hornus, *It Is Not Lawful*, p. 183.

[49]Ibid., pp. 158-212. The title of Hornus's book is a quotation from St. Martin, a soldier who left the army ca A.D. 356 after becoming a Christian and hence a "soldier of God."

[50]*Didache* 1-2, 5; *Epistle of Barnabas* 19; Athenagoras *Legatio* 35; Tertullian *Apology* 9. 1.

[51]Both Hornus, *It Is Not Lawful*, p. 113, and Durland, *No King but Caesar?* pp. 23, 24, 73, 88, 132 and 165 mention the early church's connection of abortion with violence.

[52]Bainton, *Christian Attitudes*, p. 96, notes that Augustine reduced nonresistance to an inward attitude and redefined Christian love and justice to be compatible with killing. He discusses Ambrose on pp. 89-91. Both men opposed abortion but defended the just war.

Chapter 7: The Relevance of the Early Church for Today

[1]Daniel Jenkins, in a lecture at Princeton Theological Seminary, April 23, 1982.

[2]Cadoux, *Early Christian Attitude*, p. 2.

[3]Christians were well known for their concern for orphans, but they did not, as far as we know, think to offer their love and homes to unwanted children who would otherwise have been destroyed.

[4]See Donald Granberg, "What Does It Mean to Be Pro-Life?" *Christian Century* (May 12, 1982), pp. 562-66.

[5]Mary Meehan, "Will Somebody Please Be Consistent," *Sojourners* (November

1980), p. 14.

[6]The term is from the book by John Powell, *Abortion: The Silent Holocaust* (Allen, Texas: Argus Communications, 1981).

[7]Meehan mentions the following groups: Prolifers for Survival, 345 East 9th St., Erie, PA 16503; Feminists for Life, 1503 North 47th St., Milwaukee, WI 53208; The National Youth Pro-Life Coalition, P.O. Box 67, Newport, KY 41072.

[8]Both early and modern Christian proponents of the just war theory reject the use of weapons which kill indiscriminately. One may appeal to Augustine for a defense of just war but not for a defense of nuclear weapons.

[9]Doug Badger, "Divinely Knit," *Sojourners* (November 1980), p. 17.

[10]Cathy Stentzel, "A Quiet Conversion," *Sojourners* (November 1980), p. 6.

[11]Basil *Letter* 188. 2.

[12]Service-oriented agencies related to the pro-life movement include Birthright, Bethany Christian Services and the Pregnancy Crisis Centers of the Christian Action Council. Many more are needed.

SUGGESTED READING:
SECONDARY SOURCES

(The more technical works are marked *; for primary sources, consult the index.)

*Aptowitzer, V. "Observations on the Criminal Law of the Jews." *Jewish Quarterly Review* 15 (1924): 55-118.

Bainton, Roland H. *Christian Attitudes toward War and Peace*. Nashville: Abingdon, 1960.

Brown, Harold O. J. "What the Supreme Court Didn't Know." *Human Life Review* 1, no. 2 (Spring 1975): pp. 5-21.

Cadbury, Henry J. "The Basis of Early Christian Anti-Militarism." *Journal of Biblical Literature* 37 (1918): 66-94.

Cadoux, C. John. *The Early Christian Attitude to War*. London: Headley Bros., 1919.

Cameron, A. "The Exposure of Children and Greek Ethics." *The Classical Review* 46, no. 3 (July 1932): pp. 105-14.

*Crahay, R. "Les Moralistes Anciens et l'Avortement." *L'Antiquité Classique* 10 (1941): 9-23.

Dölger, Franz. "Das Lebensrecht des ungeborenen Kindes und die Fruchtabtreibung in der Bewertung der heidnischen und christlichen Antike." In *Antike und Christentum*, Band IV, pp. 1-6. Münster: Aschendorffsche Verlagsbuchhandlung, 1934.

Durland, William R. *No King but Caesar? A Catholic Lawyer Looks at Christian Violence*. Scottdale, Pa.: Herald Press, 1975.

Feldman, David. *Birth Control in Jewish Law*. New York: New York University Press, 1968.

Ferguson, Everett. *Early Christians Speak: Faith and Life in the First Three Centuries*. Austin, Tex.: Sweet Publishing Company, 1971.

Granberg, Donald. "What Does It Mean to Be 'Pro-Life'?" *Christian Century*, May 12, 1982, pp. 562-66.

Grisez, Germain G. *Abortion: The Myths, the Realities, and the Arguments*. New York: Corpus Books, 1970.

Hornus, Jean-Michel. *It Is Not Lawful for Me to Fight: Early Christian Attitudes toward War, Violence, and the State*. Rev. ed. Translated by Alan Kreider and Oliver Coburn. Scottdale, Pa.: Herald Press, 1980.

Huser, Roger John. *Crime of Abortion in Canon Law: An Historical Synopsis and Commentary*. Washington, D.C.: Catholic University Press, 1942.

Noonan, John T., Jr. "An Almost Absolute Value in History." In John T. Noonan, Jr., ed. *The Morality of Abortion: Legal and Historical Perspectives*. Cambridge, Mass.: Belknap Press, 1970, pp. 1-59.

——————. *Contraception: A History of Its Treatment by the Catholic Theologians and Canonists*. Cambridge, Mass.: Belknap Press, 1965.

Powell, John. *Abortion: The Silent Holocaust*. Allen, Tex.: Argus Communications, 1981.

Sojourners, November 1980.

Waszink, J. H. "Abtreibung." *Reallexikon für Antike und Christentum*. Vol. 1. Stuttgart: Hiersemann Verlag, 1950, pp. 55-60.

Index of Ancient Names and Writings